Tom Philbin's
Costwise Bathroom Remodeling

A Guide to Renovating
or Improving Your Bath

Tom Philbin's Costwise Bathroom Remodeling

A Guide to Renovating or Improving Your Bath

Tom Philbin

John Wiley & Sons, Inc.
New York • Chichester • Brisbane • Toronto • Singapore

Copyright © 1992 by Tom Philbin

Published by John Wiley & Sons, Inc.

Library of Congress Cataloging in Publication Data

Philbin, Tom, 1934–
    Tom Philbin's Costwise Bathroom Remodeling: A Guide to Renovating or Improving
    Your Bath by Tom Philbin.
        p.   cm.
    Includes bibliographical references.
    ISBN 0-471-52896-X (pbk. : alk. paper)
    1. Bathrooms—Remodeling.   2. Bathrooms—Remodeling—Costs.
    I. Title.
    TH4816.3.B37P45   1991
    643'.52—dc20   91-11573

Printed in the United States of America

10 9 8 7 6 5 4 3 2

This book is warmly dedicated to Mark Rutter,
a home improvement contractor—and friend—
who emphatically makes a lie of the idea that all
home improvement contractors are incompetent—
or larcenous.

Contents

Preface

Unlike many other bathroom remodeling books on the market, this book is for people who own ordinary homes and operate on a budget. Whether you are doing a major bathroom overhaul or some minor remodeling, whether you're doing the work yourself or having it done professionally—this book is for you.

Our aim is to be realistic. All the information is based on what is possible and practical: the real space available, how much the work is really going to cost, and how to save money at every step without sacrificing workmanship or esthetics.

How many times have you picked up a book or magazine on bathroom remodeling and seen bathrooms that are literally the size of a comfortable living room—complete with dressing room, huge double vanity, sunken whirlpool, shower, storage space, workout equipment, and more? Such coffee-table depictions have little to do with what is possible or realistic for most people. The fact is, the average bathroom in the United States is 5 feet by 7 feet (indeed, contracting expert Walt Stoeppelwerth says that before 1953, *all* bathrooms were 5 by 7, with some "opulent" ones being 5 by 8).

According to National Kitchen and Bath Association (NKBA) surveys of their Certified Bath Designer members, who traditionally prefer profit-oriented larger jobs, most of the jobs they did in 1990 involved remodeling of bathrooms smaller than those commonly shown in the literature. In fact, 33 percent of their jobs were done in bathrooms of 35 to 75 square feet. And while many of the bathrooms that you see in the literature could easily cost $100,000 or more, the NKBA reports that the largest remodeling jobs—such as gutting an existing bathroom and starting over—cost no more than $8,000 to $9,000. In fact, some 60 percent of the jobs cost $2,000 or less.

Obviously, most people don't have the money to implement the technicolor fantasies usually shown.

Another misrepresentation (indeed, we think it's a ripoff) is books and articles that purport to teach inexperienced people how to be bathroom designers—to do complete remodeling jobs—in one easy lesson. One lovely four-color bathroom book we see for sale in home centers is typical. Just break out your sharpened pencils and ruler, it says, follow the simple directions, and redesign your bathroom. The unsuspecting buyer, seeing sketches and grids and technical-looking material, falls for it.

Nothing could be more unrealistic. Such remodeling—where fixtures are moved around or a bathroom is built from scratch in a new location—is not a task for the inexperienced homeowner. There are just too many variables, and those variables must blend together in a design that works. For example, if you were gutting an existing bathroom and redoing it, here's a partial list of some of the things you'd have to know—and be able to implement: how the relocated fixtures are going to tie into new and existing plumbing; lighting; ventilation; storage; wall, ceiling, and flooring materials; mirrors; safety precautions. And since it's such a small space, a bathroom is unforgiving of error. Put the edge of the tub too close to the door and you'll regret it every time the door bangs into it.

This book does not say that it will make anyone a professional bathroom technician. But it does provide vital information that will hopefully help you focus on what you need, want, and can afford in any remodeling you undertake. If you talk to a pro, you'll be able to give him or her a good idea of what's right for you. If you do it yourself, you'll have a good idea of just how much you want to do—and what you *can* do.

The information provided is comprehensive, covering everything from how various bathroom systems work to doing—or having done—a complete remodeling job. To get the most out of the book, we suggest that you read it through from the start, even if you have only a small job to do. Bathroom elements have a way of impacting on one another: you can't do one thing without it affecting another. For example, maybe you only want to replace a toilet. You should be aware that getting a toilet to match the color of other fixtures may be very difficult. To keep design harmony, you may have to replace all the fixtures.

A read-through may also expose deficiencies in your current bathroom that you didn't even know you had. For example, as you stand up after taking a bath, do you grip the soap dish handle to steady yourself? If you do, you're a prime candidate for an accident. There should be a grab bar there—and it should be screwed into the studs.

Of course, you may wonder what you can afford. After each major section there is a detailed chapter on the average costs of many jobs—from replacing a faucet to installing a light fixture to doing a total tearout and rebuilding from scratch.

You'll also find out *why* you should buy particular products or materials. Every product and material in the book is examined from the point of view of quality. You may or may not be able to afford a top-of-the-line item—but you'll know why you buy what you buy. And your knowledge can also serve as a hedge against someone selling you a low-quality item for high-quality prices.

Every chapter is suffused with concern for the cost of things. For example, Chapter 30, Where to Borrow the Money, has a complete list—and analysis—of money-lending sources. The advice in this chapter alone can save you hundreds, even thousands, of dollars.

Last, but certainly not least, there is a section on hiring people to do the work, if that's what you decide to do. Horror stories (unfortunately true) about contractors abound, but there is one perception that is dead wrong: when you hire a contractor you are at his or her mercy.

If you're willing to do a little work up front in selecting and checking out the contractor, and if you keep control of the money, you will *never* lose a large amount of money on your bathroom job. You will stay in *control* of the job itself. That's a promise.

TOM PHILBIN

Acknowledgments

My thanks to all the folks who helped me with this book, particularly, Mark Rutter, CBD; Alice Herrold; Linda Banis; Ruth Tudor; and Ellen Cheever, CBD, author of a fine book for professional bath designers, *The Basics of Bathroom Design . . . and Beyond*. Ellen graciously let me use a number of illustrations from that book. I am also grateful to the folks at Genova Products for use of a number of helpful illustrations and last, but certainly not least, to: Imagine Photography and my son Tom for all the fine photos he supplied.

Part 1

THE BASICS

Before beginning to remodel or repair your bathroom, it's a good idea to understand how a bathroom works. This section tells how the plumbing and electrical systems work, how a bathroom is constructed, and how design figures into things. It also gives you an idea of how much the various operations are going to cost . . . and how to save some money on installation without adversely affecting the result.

1

Plumbing

The most fundamental of all bathroom elements is the plumbing system. It actually consists of two separate systems: the water system and the waste system.

WATER SYSTEM

Water usually starts its journey to the home at a water processing plant, though it may also come from a well. At the plant the water is chemically purified and then is pumped out under pressure to the home. A well will have its own pump and there will be a storage tank in the home. The water travels through a main pipe until it reaches another main pipe that branches off into the house. (See Figure 1–1.)

Inside, the water passes through a meter, where its use is recorded, and then is fed into two different pipes, one for hot water and one for cold. The hot water pipe passes the water through a boiler or water heater, where it is heated, then continues its journey, traveling side by side with the cold water pipe throughout the house. Lines lead off from these pipes to the rooms where the fixtures or water-using devices (toilet, tub, sink, and so on) are located. The plumbing without the fixtures connected is known as "rough plumbing"; when plumbers speak of "roughing in" the plumbing this is what they mean. All fixtures have standard rough-in dimensions, meaning that corresponding pipes must be located at certain points so they can be connected to the fixtures. For example, the drain line for a lavatory would be 11 inches off the floor, while the water lines would each be at another height.

Water Pressure

All water travels under pressure, which is measured in pounds per square inch (psi). In the average home the pressure ranges from 20 to 45 psi. Knowing the water pressure is important when changing or adding fixtures. For example, if new fixtures are being installed on a second floor, the installer must make sure that the pressure is strong enough to push the water to the height needed.

The amount of water, or gallonage, delivered must also be checked. Pipes have to be big enough to supply enough water to existing as well as new fixtures. Sometimes existing pipe sizes can't do this, and they have to be enlarged.

Pipes that are installed vertically are called risers, and those that run horizontally are called branch lines.

Sizes and Materials

Pipe is always measured by its inside diameter; 1/2-in. pipe means its inside diameter is 1/2 in. The main line coming to the house is usually 1 1/4 or 1 1/2 in., while the branch water lines are 3/4 in. (See Figure 1–2.)

Pipe may be copper, galvanized steel, brass, or plastic, depending on where you live, the age of your home, the quality of the local water, and what local plumbing codes allow (see box).

Older homes use a lot of galvanized steel pipe, but this material has come into disfavor because of its tendency to rust and corrode; galvanized pipe uses threaded joints, which are more subject to leaks than are unthreaded joints.

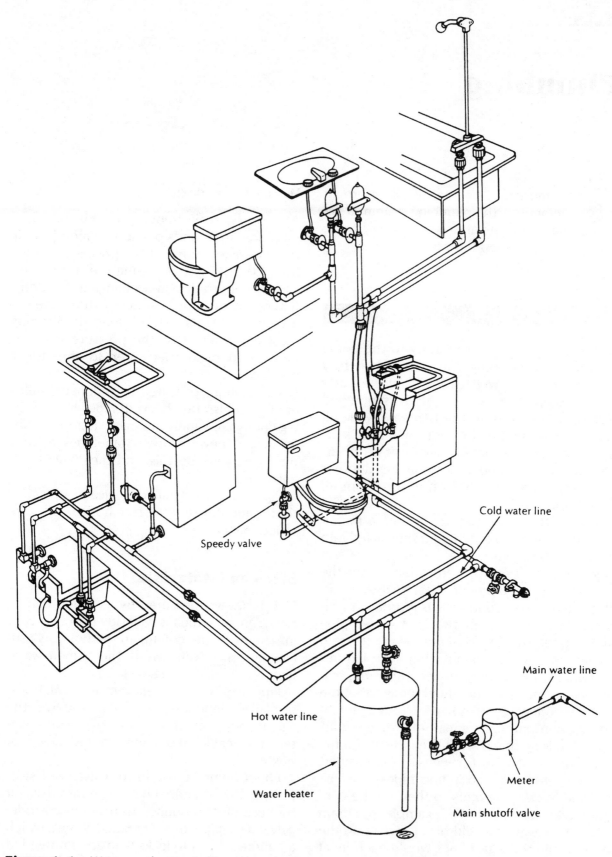

Figure 1–1.   Water supply system. (Genova Products, Inc.)

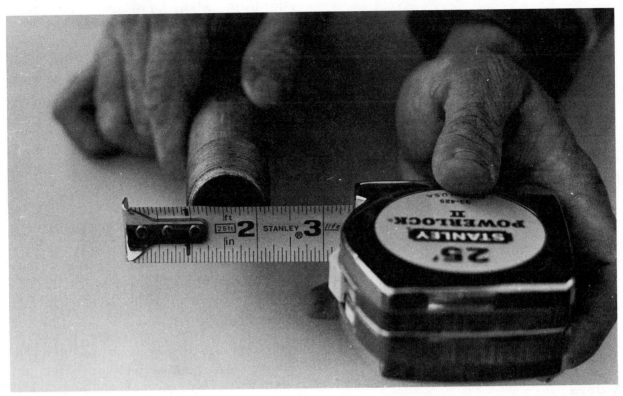

Figure 1-2. Pipe is measured according to its inside diameter. (T. Philbin III)

Building Codes

Most towns in the United States have building codes to protect the people who use the house or the systems in it from getting hurt—or worse. Some jobs require whoever is doing the work—carpenter, plumber, electrician, or do-it-yourselfer—to get a permit to do it and pay a fee for obtaining the permit. Permits are usually required only for large jobs—say, a complete bathroom remodeling.

Who may do the work is another question. In some communities you must be licensed; in others, you needn't be, but you must have a town official inspect the work once it is completed. And in some communities some jobs don't have to be looked at at all.

What you call a thing can cost—or not. Repairs generally do not change the assessed value of a house—thereby raising your taxes—but improvements do. So if you're doing a new bathroom, make sure you specify that you're making a repair, rather than a cosmetic improvement. Your tax bill will show the difference.

Brass pipe is also threaded—and equally subject to leaks.

Copper is the preferred material for water pipes and is considered the Cadillac of the industry.

In the last fifteen years or so, plastic has come into common use, but not everywhere. Most towns in the United States have plumbing codes, but some do not allow plastic to be used—if you are doing it yourself, and plastic is allowed, you're likely to find it the easiest material to work with. Just check with your local building code.

Fittings

As it wends its way through the home, water pipe obviously must take various turns, each of which calls for a fitting. Fittings are formed sections into which pipe ends are slipped. An ell fitting—shaped like the letter L—is typical; one pipe is inserted in one end of the ell and another pipe in the other end. Many other shapes allow pipe to take any direction at whatever angle is needed. (See Figure 1-3.)

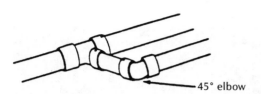

45° elbow

Figure 1-3. Fittings allow pipe to make turns.

The type of pipe dictates how the pipe is worked. Galvanized pipe is cut with a hacksaw or special cutter; the ends are then threaded (some come prethreaded) and are screwed into fittings after pipe dope or Teflon tape is applied for watertightness. Copper pipe and fittings are "sweated" together, which means that solder is melted with a flame to join the parts. Copper may be cut with a hacksaw or with a special cutter. Plastic pipe is the easiest to work with. It can be cut easily with a hacksaw and is joined to fittings with adhesive.

Valves

All water pipe systems have valves whose function is to control the water supply as needed. This allows you to make repairs on a specific section of pipe without turning off the entire system, by turning off the main valve, located at the water meter.

Valves are also located under individual fixtures and allow you to repair the fixture without turning off the main valve or one of the pipe valves. Valves are typically located under sinks, lavatories (bathroom sinks), and toilet tanks.

Such valves, commonly known as Speedy valves, are usually not terribly strong, so leaks may occur or the valves may become inoperable because of corrosion. It makes good economic sense, if you're installing a new bathroom, to provide good valves on the hot and cold risers that provide water to all the fixtures; indeed, a valve on each floor is an excellent idea. Then, when you need to work on one of the fixtures it's easy to shut off the water flow to the affected floor. You don't have to rely on the Speedy valve, which might have corroded, or be forced to turn off

water to the whole house while the repairs are made.

Faucets are the ultimate valves: turning one on or off controls the water flow at the point of use; they are the most elaborate valves you can buy. In the trade faucets are referred to as valves.

The typical water system will also have devices for coping with water hammer, a problem that occurs when rapidly moving water is brought to a sudden stop.

WASTE SYSTEM

The waste system in the house is known as the drain-waste-vent (DWV) system or, technically, as the sanitary drainage system. (See Figure 1-4.)

The spine of the DWV system is the soil stack, a 3- or 4-in. pipe that runs vertically from the lowest point in the house to the roof (a foot or so of it projects above the roof) and into which all drain and waste lines empty. If the lines are connected to sinks, lavatories, or tubs, they are called drain lines. Any line that comes from a toilet is called a waste or soil line. Lines from the toilet to the stack, called closet bends, are short and large in diameter; drain lines are usually smaller, $1\frac{1}{4}$ to 2 in. in diameter.

In some larger homes there is a secondary stack that acts just the way the primary stack does. The secondary stack handles water and waste from fixtures too far away from the primary stack to empty into it.

Venting

Stacks handle liquid waste but also have a venting function, providing air to the system and bleeding off noxious gases. The portion of the pipe below the highest fixture in the house handles waste, while the portion of the pipe above is "dry"—it functions only as a vent. (See Figure 1-5.)

In some homes additional vent-only pipes are used. These are narrow vertical pipes connected to drain and waste lines; they

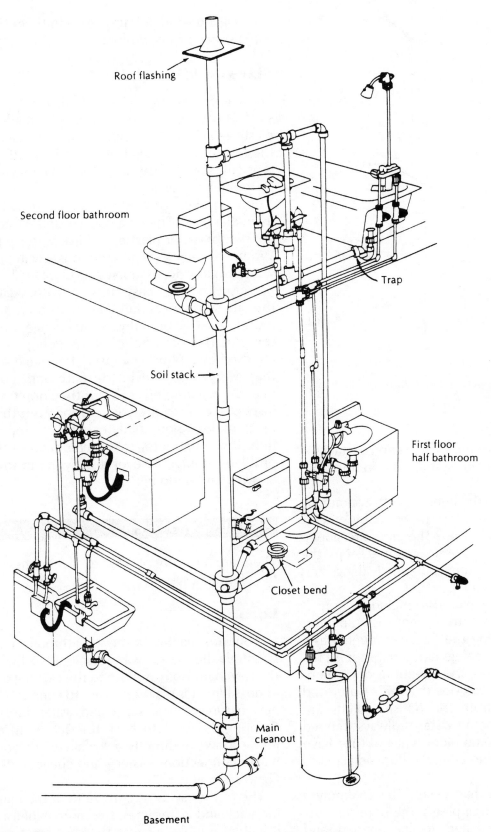

Roof flashing

Second floor bathroom

Trap

Soil stack →

First floor
half bathroom

Closet bend

Main
cleanout

Basement

Figure 1-4. Drainage-waste-vent system. (Genova Products, Inc.)

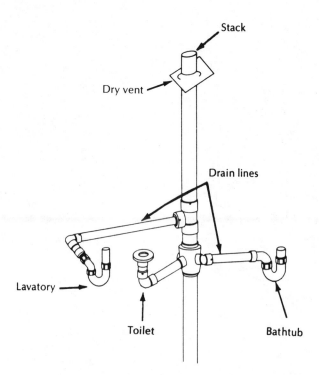

Stack

Dry vent

Drain lines

Lavatory

Toilet

Bathtub

Figure 1–5. The part of the stack above where waste drains is called a dry vent.

work just like the vent-only portion of stacks—providing air to the system and venting out the gases.

Unlike the water lines, which operate by pressure, the DWV system works by gravity. All waste moves because the pipes are sloped downward. Atmospheric pressure keeps the waste down, preventing potentially dangerous vacuums from forming.

The DWV system also includes "traps," which are designed to prevent gases and vermin from entering the house through waste and drain line openings at the fixtures. All fixtures have traps—curved sections of pipe under sinks and lavatories that trap water and seal gases off from the house. Toilets are shaped so that some water is always trapped after flushing. Some older types of tubs have "drum" traps mounted in the floor adjacent to the tub.

The stack also has a trap. This is simply a U-shaped section of pipe at the bottom.

Traps are designed to be opened and probed to clear any blockages. Because of their curved shape, things are more likely to

get snagged—indeed, trapped—in them than along straight runs of pipe.

Sizes and Materials

The stack is usually 3 to 4 in. in diameter. The stack is usually cast iron but can be made of plastic or copper, depending on what's used in the rest of the house. The closet bend (the L) is usually made of cast iron, though it may also be copper or plastic.

Branch lines for waste water are usually 2 in. in diameter. They may be galvanized steel, copper, brass, or plastic, just like water pipe. When replacing pipe sections—water or waste—many do-it-yourselfers choose plastic because it's fairly easy to work with. Again, though, some local building codes do not allow plastic. (Incidentally, if you change something in the bathroom that is going to be checked by a plumbing inspector, make sure that everything else in the bathroom complies with plumbing codes. If they don't, the inspector can require you to bring everything up to code, a potentially expensive proposition. One contractor told us he handles this problem simply: "I never let anyone in town know what I'm doing!").

SAVING MONEY

There are a variety of ways to save money on the plumbing system.

Location

If you are having a new bathroom constructed, the classic way to save is to locate the new bathroom as close to the existing one as possible. This makes it easier to connect the new fixtures to the stack and water supply. Creating a new bath back to back with, directly above, or directly below an existing one makes connections easier—and cheaper. (See Figures 1–6 and 1–7.)

The farther away you move from the existing stack and water lines, the more expensive it will be, simply because the contractor may have to cut through framing members to run water and waste lines.

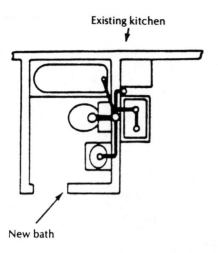

Existing kitchen

New bath

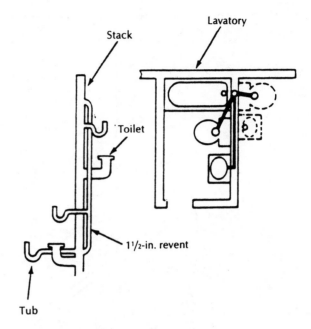

Stack

Lavatory

Toilet

1½-in. revent

Tub

Figure 1–7. Here, the plumbing is all in a compact group on both stories of the house.

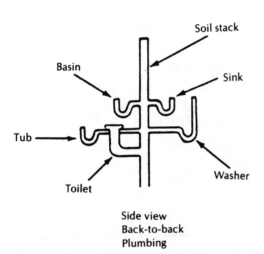

Soil stack

Basin

Sink

Tub

Toilet

Washer

Side view
Back-to-back
Plumbing

Figure 1–6. Putting the bathroom back to back with the kitchen saves money because the route from the bathroom fixtures to the plumbing is shorter.

Imagine, for a moment, an extreme situation, where the new bathroom would be located on the side of the house opposite from the existing stack and supply lines. In this case it probably wouldn't be feasible to go through the existing framing crosswise; it would be cheaper—though not by any means cheap—to run a line from the basement up.

Minimize Cutting of Framing

One good way to save money, if a new stack is needed, is to run pipe so that only minimal cutting of framing is required. For example, you may be able to run pipe up inside closets or boxed into a corner, or make a cutout in

bookcase shelves and run pipe behind them. The idea is not to run it up inside walls; that's when it gets expensive.

If another stack is installed, the contractor should make sure that it can be tied into the main drain. The connecting pipe must pitch (slope) ¼ in. to the foot. Therefore, the connecting pipe should be connected to the new stack in such a way that it can traverse the distance between the two stacks and maintain proper pitch.

**Lavatory and Shower
Easier to Move**

If you want to move fixtures within a bathroom, it is usually much cheaper to move the lavatory or shower than the toilet because of the way they're framed. The lavatory and shower have water supply connections inside the wall, where there is space to move the lines; the drain also goes into the wall. A shower may also be easier to move, depending on the way it is hooked up. Sometimes it is and sometimes it isn't.

A toilet, however, is always difficult to move because it is tied into joists, which are floor framing members (see Chapter 3). Moving a

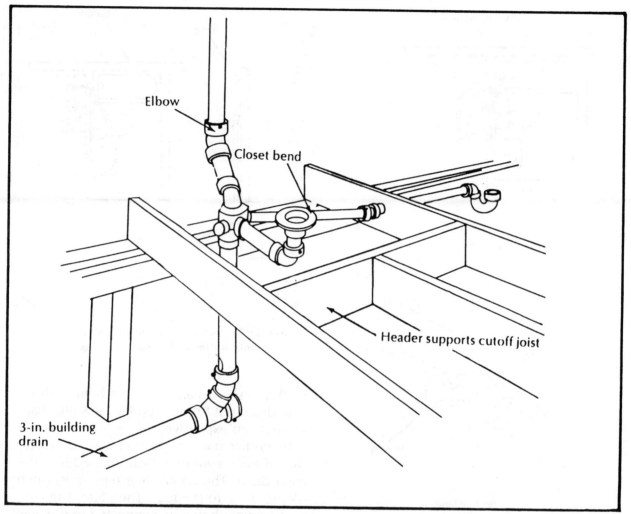

Elbow

Closet bend

Header supports cutoff joist

3-in. building
drain

Figure 1–8.   Moving a toilet is expensive because framing, shown here, must be cut through to move the closet flange (bend) to align it with the new toilet location. (Genova Products, Inc.)

toilet often involves cutting through the joists and providing new support boards—"sister joists," as plumbers say. This is expensive. (See Figure 1–8.)

Moving a tub is also expensive because you're going to have to reframe for it.

Replacing Two-Piece Toilet Cheaper

Toilets, which will be discussed in Chapter 7, come in one- and two-piece styles, meaning that the water tank is either built into the toilet or is separate.

A one-piece toilet is a sleek, low-slung unit that requires a lower water line than a two-

piece toilet. If you replace a two-piece with a one-piece toilet, it will be more expensive because the water supply pipes will have to be lowered. It is cheaper to replace a two-piece toilet with the same model; then water supply pipes can stay in the same position. (See Figures 1–9 and 1–10.)

If you live in an old house, the rough-in dimension—the distance to the wall from the center of where the toilet is bolted to the floor—may be 10 in. or 14 in. The problem is that modern toilets have a 12-in. rough-in dimension. If you try to use the 12-in. dimension you may have to move the closet bend and modify framing, and this can be expensive. A more economical solution is to find

Figure 1-9. Two-piece toilet—the tank is on the back.

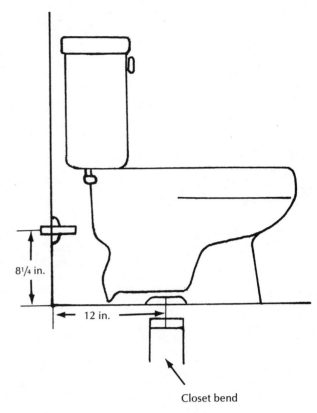

8¼ in.

12 in.

Closet bend

Figure 1-11. Rough-in for a toilet is usually 12 in., which means from the wall to the center of the closet bend.

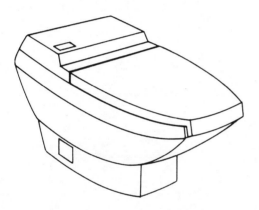

Figure 1-10. One-piece toilet. It costs more than the two-piece.

and install a toilet that has the existing rough-in dimension (10 in. or 14 in.). (See Figure 1-11.)

Saving Water

As bathroom designer and remodeling contractor Mark Rutter put it: "You don't need to stand under Niagara Falls to take a shower." Mark was referring to the showerheads some people use that spew out unnecessary amounts of water. As will be detailed in Chapter 10, you needn't use such showerheads—and over the long run you can save hundreds of dollars.

The same is true of toilets. Years ago, 5 gallons of water were required to flush a toilet. Today as little as 1.5 gallons may be used (see Chapter 7).

2

The Electrical System

If fixtures are to be moved within your bathroom or an entirely new bathroom is being created, the electrical system will most likely need to be modified, because lights and power outlets (for shavers and the like) will have to be rearranged.

HOW IT WORKS

The electrical system of a home is rather like a plumbing system, but instead of water going through pipes, the electrical current goes through wire. (See Figure 2–1.) In order to flow, electricity needs a circuit—a closed wire loop that goes around and around: when the circuit is interrupted, so is the electricity.

Electricity is created at the power company by the action of huge magnets. Like water, it is pushed out—in this case along high-tension wires (the topmost wires strung between telephone poles)—and is then tapped by a main wire to the house, called the service entrance cable.

As with water, the cable is routed through a meter where power use is recorded. Inside the house, the wire is divided up, at what is known as a bus bar, into individual circuits. Circuit wires go through walls and ceilings to the receptacles or switches, where electricity is tapped off for use. Individual circuits are not usually linked to one specific room, but rather are run according to what is most efficient when the house is being built. Part of one circuit may be in the bathroom, part in a bedroom, and part in the kitchen. Electrical routing can seem mysterious—but it made economic sense to the electrician who put it in.

Wire is technically known as a conductor. It is composed of copper covered with insulation and then covered with either a ribbed metal casing called "BX" or a plastic casing called "Romex." (Both are brand names.) (See Figure 2–2.)

Wire is classified according to its gauge: the larger the gauge number, the thinner the wire and the less current it can carry; the smaller the number, the thicker the wire and the more current it can carry. Number 38 wire, for example, is as thin as a hair; number 2 wire is as thick as a pencil. Number 14 wire, which is used for most circuits in the home, is about the diameter of the head of a pin. Large appliances, such as refrigerators and stoves, need more current than the average device, such as a lamp, and therefore heavier wire—number 12—is used.

TERMS

Like water, electricity travels through the wire at a certain pressure. The rate of flow is measured in volts. In house wiring this is 117 to 120 volts, commonly called 110, or 240 volts, commonly called 220. (The lower figures are used because voltages from the power company vary, but the minimums are 110 and 220.) The voltages required for different appliances vary. Large appliances need 220 volts while lights and small appliances need only 110 volts to push the electricity through the wire.

As water's flow through pipes is measured at a certain gallonage (gallons per minute), electricity's flow through wires is measured at a certain amperage, or amps. Different circuits need different amperages. For lights, 15

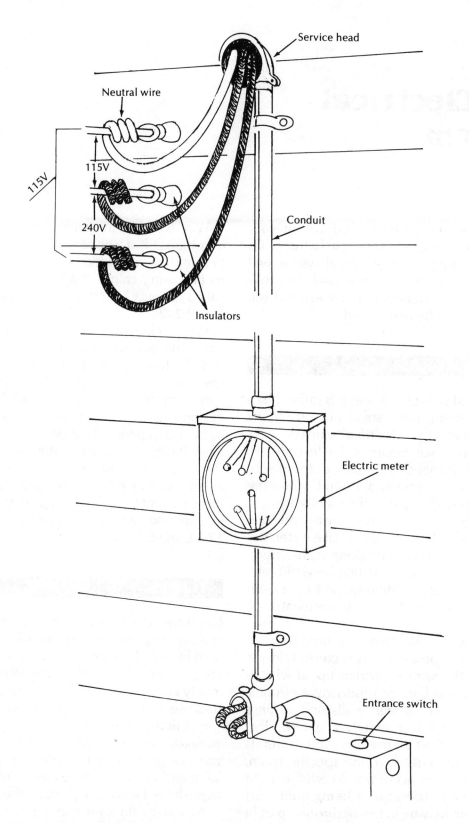

Neutral wire

115V

115V

240V

Service head

Conduit

Insulators

Electric meter

Entrance switch

Figure 2–1.   Power comes into the house through a service head, then travels down and through a meter, where its use is recorded.

Figure 2–2. BX wire (left) and Romex (right), the most common house wiring. (T. Philbin III)

amps is usually used; large appliances need 20 to 50 amps. One large appliance, say a stove, may need its own circuit; this is called a dedicated circuit. Older homes have a capacity of only 60 amps, while newer ones, with greater electrical needs brought on by modern technology, commonly have 150 amps.

The power used in terms of both amperage and voltage is measured in watts. To determine watts used, multiply amps times volts. If an appliance drew $1/2$ amp at 110 volts, for example, it would use 55 watts; if it drew 2 amps at 110 volts it would use 220 watts.

SAFETY

Fuses and Circuit Breakers

The key devices used to protect against fire are fuses and circuit breakers. Fuses—round screw-in devices—are usually found in older homes, while circuit breakers, which turn on and off like a switch, are used in newer homes.

Each circuit is protected by either a fuse or a circuit breaker of a specific amperage. If for some reason a circuit is forced to carry too much current (amperage), the fuse or circuit breaker, which is mechanically—metallically—part of the circuit, will "blow" or "trip," thereby shutting down the circuit. Were it not for this feature, the wires could overload, heating up to the point where a fire could occur.

Grounding

Grounding is another key safety principle. The term derives from a simple fact: the natural path electricity takes is to the ground. Consider, for example, a bolt of lightning: it starts in the sky, but shoots down toward and into the ground.

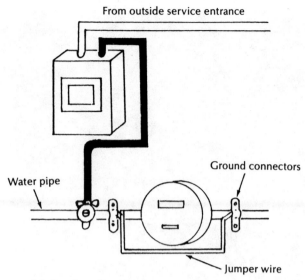

Figure 2–3. One way to ground the house. Electricity travels down to the water pipe, where it then travels on a jumper wire over the meter to the pipe again and then down into the ground.

All electric devices that carry significant amperage or current must be grounded. Indeed, the house itself is grounded. This is done by establishing a path that lightning will take to the ground rather than going through the house itself—and destroying it.

When building a house a builder, who knows as well as you and I that metal is a great conductor of electricity, will make some provision for grounding. (See Figure 2–3.) In some cases this is a copper rod driven into the ground, to which all the wires lead. (See Figure 2–4.) Lightning striking the house would hit

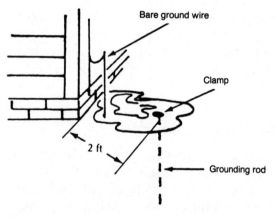

Figure 2–4. Another way to ground the house.

the wires and travel down them, through the rod, and into the ground. In other cases there may be a separate lightning rod on the house.

Grounding Wires

Appliances are grounded by means of a grounding wire, which is the third wire on an appliance. If there is an electrical malfunction and electricity leaks, it will follow the path of the third wire down the cord, into the circuit, and into the ground rod. If that third wire weren't there, the electricity might follow another path to the ground—through your body. But since metal is a better conductor of electricity than is flesh and blood, the electricity takes the path of least resistance.

Lights and similar small current users don't need a third wire because only small amounts of amperage are needed to make them work: even if electricity were to run through you, you'd get a mild shock rather than being seriously hurt—or worse.

Bathroom Dangers

The bathroom is probably the most dangerous room in the house, electrically speaking, because water is an excellent conductor, and in the bathroom water and electricity rub shoulders. The problem is that water helps make a better ground. If current were to run through your body while you were standing on a dry floor, it might not be strong enough to go past your feet and into the ground. But if you were standing in water, a connection would be made, and the electricity would go to ground perfectly—and probably kill you.

At any rate, safety is our byword, and we suggest a number of things in this book to increase your safety. For instance, you should put switches out of reach of the bathtub or shower; you should never be able to reach them while standing in water.

GFCI

An excellent safety device that should be part of any bathroom is a ground fault circuit

Figure 2-5.   GFCI (right) and regular outlet (left). GFCI is a safety device. (T. Philbin III)

interrupter (GFCI). There are various types; the ones for the bathroom look something like receptacles but have a reset button on them and function very differently. (See Figure 2-5.)

Electrical devices are all connected to a black wire, or hot wire, that brings the power to the device, and a white or neutral wire that returns the power to the plant. The power on these two "legs" should be equal. If there's an electrical malfunction the power balance will be upset, and the errant power will start to drain to the ground—and will go through whatever is the shortest route, including your body.

The GFCI is designed to sense this power imbalance (or ground fault) and turn the circuit off almost instantaneously—in 25/1000th of a second, which is much faster than it would go off if only a circuit breaker or fuse

tripped or blew. Fast enough, indeed, to protect you from serious shock.

You can also get GFCIs that are wired into the circuit. Whatever type you use, some kind of GFCI should be installed. In most localities building codes won't give you a choice: GFCIs must be used, or at least certain items must have them and be on dedicated circuits. Such items usually include whirlpools, saunas, steam generators, in-line heaters, and other devices where shock hazard is present.

SAVING MONEY

The same rule applies to the electrical system as to the plumbing: the more you change the system, the more it will cost. But things are relative: to run new wires is a lot easier and cheaper than to run new plumbing. For one thing, wire is flexible—it can be bent to take the path you want—and a lot smaller; you can drill holes and run wire through framing members where you couldn't run plumbing.

In some cases, dedicated (one purpose) circuits will be required, but if not it is usually cheaper to tie electrical devices into existing circuits, simply because less cutting into walls, ceiling or flooring materials, and framing is required. To decide which devices should tie into which circuits, the electrician will have to see what circuits serve which devices and if there is room on them for other devices—such as that new ventilating fan or the vanity lights.

Like other tradespeople, electricians must be licensed and follow local codes in whatever they do. It would be a good idea to learn what these codes are: you don't want an electrician building at lower than code, but you also don't want him or her going too far—at greater expense. Of course, if reading codes seems too daunting a process, you can simply discuss things with the electrician; that is, ask if what's being done is simply up to code, or greater than code requirements—at perhaps additional expense.

3

How a Bathroom Is Built

A bathroom is built like most rooms in the home, with one important exception: measures must be taken to protect it against moisture, because in no room in the home is moisture generated to the same degree as in the bathroom.

FRAMING

As with any other room, a bathroom is first "framed out." (See Figure 3–1.) In most modern homes, this means that studs are used for walls, joists for floors, and either joists or ceiling beams for the ceiling, depending on house construction.

Studs are usually 2 × 4 boards, 8 ft high and set 16 in. on centers (o.c.), meaning they are nailed 16 in. apart from center to center. In some older homes (and even in some newer ones), the studs are 24 in. apart.

Floor framing is, as mentioned, joists. These are simply large (2 × 10) boards that are nailed side by side 16 in. or 24 in. apart.

In a one-story home without an attic, the ceiling beams, also nailed 16 in. apart, will be 2 × 4s. If there is a second floor or an attic, there will be joists: 2 × 8 or 2 × 10 members that are strong enough to walk on.

Bathroom framing will include horizontal crosspieces called headers placed between the studs, on which the water piping is mounted. There will also be headers that form a rectangular recess for a built-in medicine chest, as well as cleats to support the tub flange or lip.

WALL, CEILING, AND FLOORING MATERIALS

Sheetrock

In a bathroom, as well as in other rooms in the house, the wall material used most frequently is Sheetrock, a brand name for plasterboard. This comes in various thicknesses and sizes, but 1/2-in.-thick, 4- × 8-ft panels are usually used. The panels are simply cut to size and nailed to the studs, and then the seams are sealed with perforated tape covered by a number of smoothed layers of joint compound.

In the tub and/or shower area, a special water-resistant Sheetrock is used. (See Figure 3–2.) This is known in the trade as "greenboard" (regular Sheetrock is white) after the color of the water-resistant paper facing.

In recent years two other materials, which are said to be even more resistant to water, have been increasingly used. These are cement board, such as that made by Durock, and Wonderboard. They are only a little more expensive than Sheetrock and more than make up the difference in water resistance. (See Figure 3–3.)

Standard Sheetrock is normally used on the ceiling.

Plaster

In older bathrooms, walls and ceilings will usually be made of plaster. This is wet plaster

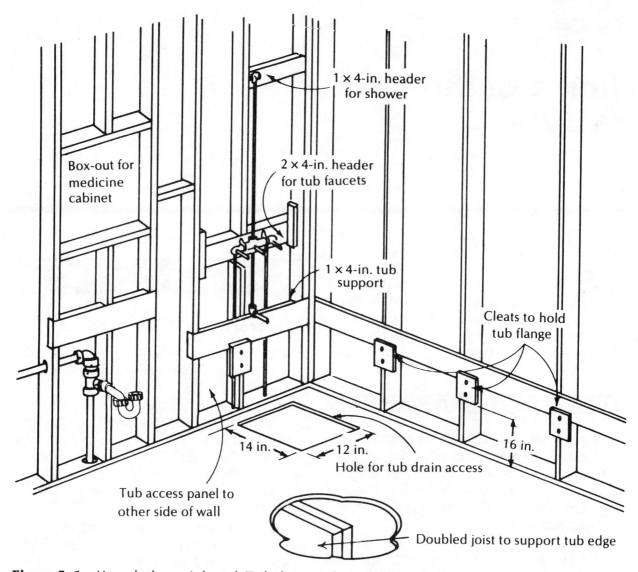

Box-out for medicine cabinet

1 × 4-in. header for shower

2 × 4-in. header for tub faucets

1 × 4-in. tub support

Cleats to hold tub flange

14 in.

12 in.

16 in.

Hole for tub drain access

Tub access panel to other side of wall

Doubled joist to support tub edge

Figure 3–1. How a bathroom is framed. (Toilet lines not shown.) (Genova Products, Inc.)

that is applied over a lath or gypsum board base and smoothed out with a trowel. At one time this "wet wall"—as opposed to Sheetrock, which is called "drywall"—was used in most homes. But the ease of installing Sheetrock has made plaster almost obsolete.

The floor will be installed on top of a subflooring. In older homes individual tongue-and-groove boards were used (the tongue on the side of one board fits snugly into a groove on the side of its neighbor), but today plywood is most often used. Depending on what flooring material is being installed, there may also be "underlayment," which is usually just

another layer of material, such as plywood or Durock.

Rough-ins

The plumbing and electrical facilities will already have been installed before any wall, ceiling, or flooring material is in. As those materials are nailed in place, holes are cut for water and waste pipes and electrical outlets. The ends of water and waste pipes that project from the wall without the fittings or fixtures attached are called the rough plumbing or rough-in. Wires that sprout from

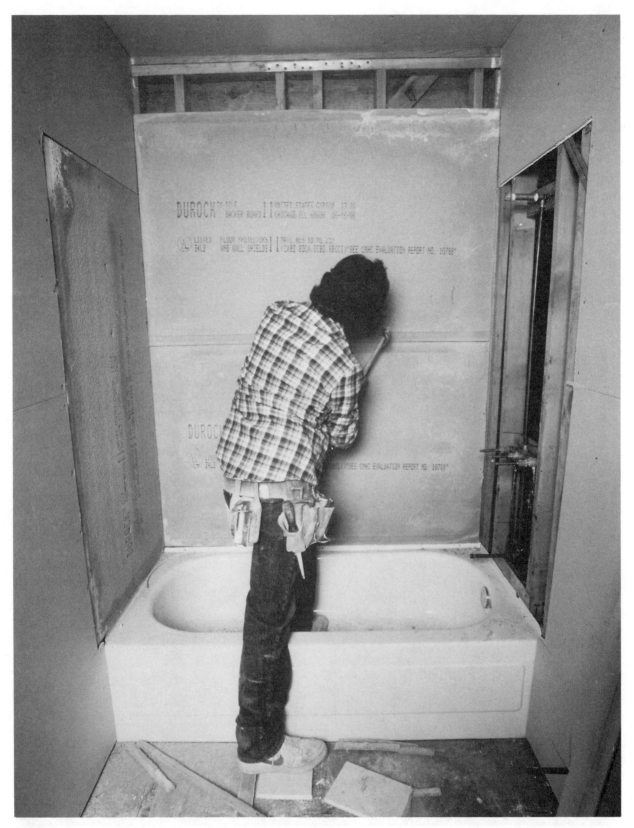

Figure 3–2. Studs are covered with water-resistant Sheetrock or, even better, Wonderboard or Durock (shown here), a cement-based product.

walls and ceilings are called the electrical rough-in.

As suggested in Chapters 1 and 2, there is nothing rough about pipe or wire locations. Their placement must be precise. For example, faucets come with certain "centers"—the distance between the center of the hot water handle and the center of the cold. (See Figure 3–4.) This might be, say, 6 in. In this case the hot and cold water pipe stubs projecting from the wall must also be 6 in. apart so that the faucets can be connected.

Similarly, drain pipe locations for the lavatory must be properly positioned, and so must the waste pipe for the toilet. Commonly, a toilet has a 12-in. rough-in, meaning that when you place the toilet flush against the wall, the

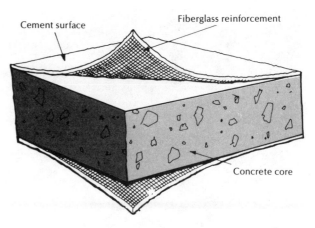

Figure 3–3.   Wonderboard.

Figure 3–4.   Faucets have centers, which is the distance between the centers of the faucet handles. This measurement is the same as the distance between the water pipe stubs below. (Kohler Co.)

distance from the center of its hole to the wall is 12 in. Hence, the closet bend's or waste pipe's center must be 12 in. from the wall.

The fixtures and other facilities are put in before finish materials are installed. Getting these in without scratching or otherwise damaging them can be tricky. (Tip: Make sure that any fixture you buy can physically fit through the halls leading to the bathroom and through the door itself. Quite a few people have bought fixtures and then learned too late that they are too big to fit.)

FINISH MATERIALS

Since finish material used in the bathroom must be water resistant, the material most often employed is a type of ceramic tile that is highly water resistant. It is used on both floors and walls—particularly walls surrounding the tub—and can be installed in a variety of ways (see Chapter 21).

A resilient sheet flooring, which is usually big enough to cover the floor without seams, is also frequently used. In fact, according to a study done in 1990 by the National Kitchen and Bath Association (NKBA), tile and vinyl dominate finish flooring: tile is used 71 percent of the time, and vinyl sheet flooring is used 27 percent of the time. Wood is used only 0.5 percent of the time, carpet 0.5 percent, and assorted others 1 percent.

Paint is also a favorite for walls and ceilings, as are wall coverings that resist moisture. (On walls, paint is used 18 percent of the time, wallpaper 57 percent, tile 23 percent, and others 2 percent.)

SAVING MONEY

If you want to completely remodel a bathroom or build a new one somewhere else in the house, you might want to think twice if it's an old house. Framing member spacing, such as 2 x 4s, was not done so precisely in some older homes, and indeed some walls were made narrower than others. Such things can make it problematic to run new pipes. More-

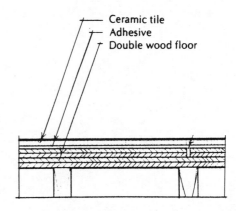

Figure 3-5. Ceramic tile installed with adhesive. The less costly way to go.

over, demolishing a plaster and lath wall is messy and expensive: it will cost twice what demolishing a Sheetrock wall can cost. You might opt for new fixtures, plumbing, and wiring but keep the walls and ceiling intact.

If you plan to use ceramic tile on the floor of a new bathroom, make sure that you have at least 1 1/2 in. of wood beneath—say, 3/4-in.-thick subfloor topped by 3/4-in. plywood and, for extra strength, they should be glued and screwed together. On such a base you can install the tile using the "thin-set" method, which describes a group of materials—adhesives and mortars—applied thinly under the tile. The "thick-set" method, or a "mud job," uses a thick bed of cement. (See Figures 3-5 and 3-6.) A thin-set job can be done much more cheaply, and the tile will never move—you won't be making expensive repairs sometime in the future.

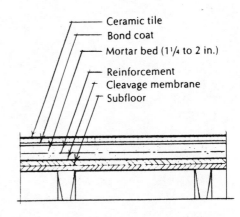

Figure 3-6. "Mud" job (the costly way to go).

4

Design

The word *design* can be used in a variety of ways, but here we mean bathroom looks in general: how all the classic elements that go into design—color, texture, shape, theme, and so on—harmonize . . . or don't.

There is no way, we feel, that anyone can learn to be a bathroom designer just by reading a book. On the other hand, a successful remodeling—whether it be simple or complex—must take into account some basic design ideas, and it is possible for the inexperienced person to keep these in mind when thinking about remodeling a bathroom yourself or in speaking with a professional about design.

This chapter includes some good design ideas, some cautions, and some sources for design ideas.

DOS AND DON'TS

Every bathroom, however small, should have a theme that produces a certain feeling. (See Figure 4–1.) It can be colonial, modernistic, high-tech, or whatever, but when you're thinking about a bathroom, don't mix apples and plums—unless you're sure they're going to work together. Don't mix colonial and modernistic, or high-tech with Victorian, to offer some extreme examples.

Try for color harmony. Certain colors go together: warm colors such as browns, yellows, and reds go together and so do cool colors such as blues and greens. A neutral color, such as white, can go with almost any color without jarring the viewer. Let one color dominate the scene; too many colors can look jumbled. Indeed, the essence of good design is simplicity. A painter once told me that when he painted

an apartment in a depressed area of New York city, every room was a different color. When he painted a ten-room Park Avenue apartment that had been decorated by a professional designer almost all the rooms were a pale blue. This ties into what Bob Hartig, a wallpaper hanger, told me: "Walls and ceiling should just be background for the design, the canvas on which you put the other colors—the colored fixtures, the shower curtains, and so forth."

Take care not to go "far out" in design. Some people will design a bathroom according to current fads—and five years down the road will regret it deeply. For example, there was a time not too long ago when bathrooms were dominated by greens, pinks, and grays. Today, though, these bathrooms look dated. According to NKBA surveys, the most popular color used in bathrooms nationwide is white (52 percent), followed by almond (24 percent), pastels (14 percent), wood tones (6 percent), gray (2 percent) and others (2 percent).

Use fixtures and, if possible, accessories from one manufacturer. There are many fixture manufacturers and, although fixtures can be bought that look alike, one manufacturer's shade of a particular color, say white, will not be the same as another's. So if you buy a white toilet from one manufacturer, a white tub from another, and a white lavatory from yet another, they will all be white, but they will be different shades—and the difference will show.

Also, if the manufacturer sells accessories—toilet tissue holders, soap dishes, glass holders, and so on—see if they have them in the same color as the fixtures. Matching fixture and accessory colors can bring unity to a bathroom. (See Figure 4–2.)

Use color to "expand" a room. Using light or even pastel colors can help make a small

Figure 4–1. Every bathroom should have a theme. This one has an almost rustic feeling. (Wood Mode)

Figure 4–2. A number of manufacturers make accessories in the same color and style. Accessories are very important to good design. (Eljer)

bathroom look bigger. Darker colors or many colors together tend to make the room look smaller.

Use mirrors to "expand" a room. (See Figure 4–3.) The French have a phrase, *trompe l'oiel*, which means "fool the eye." That's what mirrors do. Judicious placement can make a room seem larger than it is. (See Figure 4–4.)

Use complementary materials. It is difficult to lay down absolutes when it comes to suggesting materials to use, except one: they should harmonize. For example, if you used cedar siding for walls, vinyl for floors, and ceramic tile for a countertop, the textures and shapes wouldn't harmonize. Try to stick to the tried and true—what works.

IDEAS IN ACTION

To get ideas for a bathroom, nothing beats seeing the particular designs in action, and we strongly recommend that you do this. You can see right away what works and what doesn't, at least for you. Also, if the project will involve a designer or contractor who specializes in bathrooms, you will have a visual aid to communicate what you want.

Figure 4-3. Mirrors can open up a room. This mirror folds out. (Nutone)

Figure 4-4a. Cabinets with mirrored doors are shallow enough to be recessed in a wall. You can use as many cabinets as you wish, creating a wall-of-mirror effect or by leaving doors slightly open a mirror-surround effect. Hinges used are hidden. (Nutone)

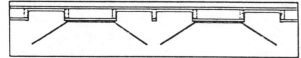

Figure 4-4b. View of cabinet arrangement from above. (Nutone)

Figure 4-4c. In small areas, a corner mirror can expand things. (Nutone)

There are a number of sources for designs, and your library can be quite an asset. It can provide you with a variety of visual models and design sources.

Magazines and Books

One such source is magazines. Libraries commonly carry magazines such as *Woman's Day, Family Circle, Better Homes & Gardens,* and others, and these periodically contain stories on bathrooms that contain a variety of color photos. Some magazines even have specific bathroom issues.

There are also a number of "special-interest" magazines that specialize in kitchens and bathrooms. Such publications are chock-full of photos and information. Your library may not carry the special-interest publications, but some other library in the system might. Most libraries today are linked together by computer, and your local librarian can tell you what other libraries in the area carry.

Note, however, that some of the ideas you'll see in such high-gloss magazines simply won't work. Sometimes such bathrooms are designed with prettiness and impact in mind—in a studio setting—without any thought as to whether or not they work. You should look at them—or have a professional designer look at them—with a careful eye. Note, too, that many of the bathroom ideas you'll find in such magazines are beyond the budgets of most people, and so will remain more fantasy than fact. Still, you may be able to fish out some good, practical ideas. (See Figures 4–5 through 4–7.)

Figure 4–5. Only J. Paul Getty could afford the above, but one can filch good ideas, such as flooring style, figurines on soffit, recessed cabinetry. (Eljer)

Figure 4–6. Decals on inexpensive fixtures and a free rein with creative ideas can prove interesting. (Mannington)

Figure 4-7.   The greenhouse effect with a more positive connotation—plants and light add much to this bathroom.

Another good source of design ideas is bathroom books. A number of books have been published over the last ten years or so that contain many feasible ideas, and many are in color. As with magazines, your local library may well be able to access anything in the entire library system.

Videos

Yet another possible source is videos, although the ideas here will be somewhat limited because they nearly all concentrate more on step-by-step, how-to instructions on various jobs than on presenting a panoply of design ideas.

Videos are available at libraries and, of course, commercially. Hometime puts out a good series on the home, a number of which are devoted to bathrooms and discuss design to some degree. You might also want to view such videos to get a highly detailed idea of how various jobs are done.

Showrooms

A good way to find out how things look is to visit bathroom showrooms. Manufacturers such as Kohler and American Standard have showrooms where they display various bathroom "vignettes." Big ceramic tile dealers also have bathroom vignettes, as do some plumbing supply houses.

Friends' Homes

You can also see finished bathrooms in the homes of friends or neighbors. Most people know someone who has had a bathroom remodeled recently, and it shouldn't be difficult to contact the person by phone and talk about the job to see if it sounds like something you'd be interested in. For example, if you call and find out that the new bathroom is all art deco, and you like colonial, then you know it's not for you. However, the new bathroom may give you ideas for storage that will work fine for you.

To gain additional specific sources for your research you can also ask people where they got their designs. If you do like a specific bathroom, ask if you can borrow a picture of it, or where you might get one (contractors often take photos of finished work). You can show such photos to a designer or contractor who gets involved in your job. These professionals will also have photos for you to look at—and lots of ideas.

Finally, of course, there is this book. Although the pictures are not in color, there are many good design ideas.

5

Costs

As mentioned in the box below, the costs given here are approximate. They will, however, give you some sense of what things cost if you have no idea at all.

Costs are given for what an overall job might cost, as well as for some specific jobs.

Unless otherwise noted, these cost estimates assume that the contractor is supplying all products and materials, which would be "builder grade"—low, but not the lowest grade. It is also assumed that the contractor would do the "tear-out"—the gutting of the existing bath.

OVERALL BATHROOM REMODELING JOB

Job Specifications

The following job specifications (specs) would apply. Costs of various sizes of bathrooms are given following these specs.

- Prepare plans (fees for permits are not included).
- Tear out all fixtures and a ceramic tile floor set in cement ("mud") and remove the debris.
- Rerough plumbing for a three-fixture bathroom with new copper water supply and new copper, plastic, or cast iron waste lines to the stack with new valves at each fixture. The three fixtures (lavatory, toilet, tub) would be builder-grade quality. The tub would be 5 ft long (standard) and would include shower fittings.
- Install new 5/8-in. plywood subfloor.
- Install new flush hollow-core door with bathroom-style lock.
- Install new 1/2-in. moisture-resistant drywall over all walls and ceilings; tape and finish same.
- Install new ceramic tile on floor with 4-in. tile base.
- Install new standard ceramic tile on walls (Wonderboard base) to a height of 6 ft above the floor.

- Install ceramic tile towel bar in tub area.
- Install new switch and light over lavatory and ground fault duplex outlet next to lavatory.
- Install recessed medicine cabinet with overhead fluorescent fixture. The cabinet would be 24 × 16 in. and have two mirror doors.
- Install chrome towel bar, paper holder, glass, and toothbrush holder.
- Paint with three coats of top-quality semi-gloss enamel.
- Remove old fixtures and rubbish from job (dumping fee not included).

Costs

As specified above, bathrooms of various sizes would cost the following:

5 × 7 ft:	$7230
5 × 9 ft:	$7455
8 × 10 ft:	$8100
10 × 10 ft:	$8600

VARIOUS JOBS: PLUMBING

- Remove toilet, lavatory, tub or shower base and cap water and waste supply lines: $66.75
- Raise existing vent stack through roof up to 10 ft: $163.50
- Install hot and cold water valves on lavatory lines: $33.00
- Hang horizontal waste line: $46.50/ft
- Replace horizontal galvanized water pipes in basement with 3/4-in. copper pipes when the ceiling is open: $900 base price plus $0.60/ft

VARIOUS JOBS: ELECTRICAL

- Install ceiling fixture, fishing wire through walls and ceiling: $141.00 (excluding fixture)
- Install one-tube, one-plug fluorescent fixture over medicine cabinet, including outlet, fixture, and switch: $262.50
- Increase electrical service to 150 amps by adding circuit breakers: $733.50
- Increase electrical service to 200 amps as above: $892.00

Part 2

FIXTURES AND FITTINGS

The core products in any bathroom are, of course, the fixtures—toilet, tub, and lavatory—and the fittings—the mechanical parts that let you operate the fixtures.

The chapters in this section provide a guide to what's available, what's good and what isn't, and some tips on how fixtures should be laid out for maximum convenience.

6

Lavatories

Lavatories—bathroom sinks—are available in a variety of colors, sizes, and qualities. The fittings for lavatories—faucets and related hardware—also come in a great variety of styles, colors, and qualities, and are bought separately from the lavatory.

MATERIALS

Most lavatories are made of enameled steel, vitreous china, cast polymer, enameled cast iron, or "solid-surface" materials such as Corian.

Enameled Steel

This is formed steel with a porcelain coating, and perhaps its only advantages are its low cost and light weight. But its big problem is chipping: if something is dropped on it it can chip and there is no feasible way to hide the blemish. In addition, water driving against this type of lavatory is noisy. The noise can be mitigated somewhat by having the steel undercoated.

Vitreous China

This is hard-glazed clay, the same material that is used to make toilets. Quality varies, depending on the quality of the clay used to manufacture the unit and the way it is fired. The sign of a good-quality vitreous china lavatory is a smooth surface free of pinholes, bubbles, or discoloration.

Cast Polymer

This term describes a variety of materials that use a polyester resin as a base, in which other materials—such as marble, granite, glass, or hydrated aluminum—are mixed to produce the final product. The surface is coated with a gel that contains the color and design. The gel is a film only; it does not go all the way through the material.

Cast polymer seeks to simulate the appearance of other materials, but it is also available in solid colors. The most popular of these is cultured marble, which resembles pure marble.

As with some plumbing products—such as fittings—it is all but impossible to judge quality in cast polymer products merely by looking. Your best bet is to make sure the product has been approved by the Cultured Marble Institute, which monitors quality.

One problem with cultured marble is that the color does not go all the way through. It is difficult to repair a damaged gel coating without the repair showing. Gel coats may be 0.0016 or 0.0020 in. thick; the thicker material, of course, is more durable.

Enameled Cast Iron

Cast iron is considered one of the best lavatory materials (contractors rate it and vitreous china equally). It consists of an extremely hard, durable (and heavy) metal coated with enamel. Because it doesn't flex, like enameled steel, it is much less likely to chip; the coating is also much thicker, making it much more resistant to chipping or denting.

Solid Surface

There are a variety of solid-surface materials, such as Avenite and Corian. Such materials are made in several different ways, but in all of them the color and/or pattern goes all the way through. If the material is scratched or otherwise damaged, an invisible repair can be made by sanding off the blemish. This cannot be done with other materials without the repair showing to some degree.

Figure 6–1. Wall-hung lavatory.

TYPES

Lavatories come in a seemingly endless variety of shapes—round, rectangular, triangular (fits nicely in a corner), square, hexagonal—ou name it. The basic types are wall-hung, pedestal, self-rimming, rimmed, undermounted, and integral. Each type has advantages and disadvantages.

Wall-Hung

As the name suggests, this type of lavatory is mounted on the wall by means of brackets that are secured to the studs. (See Figure 6–1.) If you have small children, think twice about this type. Youngsters are likely to use it as a chinning bar, with predictable results.

Pedestal

This is a one-piece lavatory consisting of the lavatory or basin mounted on a pedestal. It is strictly for use in bathrooms that have plenty of other counter space, because the pedestal lavatory has none. Since there is no vanity cabinet to hide water pipes, they show. (See Figures 6–2 and 6–3.)

Figure 6–2. The exposed plumbing shows in the pedestal-type lavatory.

Figure 6-3. Pedestal lavatory. (American Olean)

Rimmed

Here, the lavatory is mounted in a rim that is secured to a cutout made in the vanity top. The problem with this type is that soil can collect under the rim, making it difficult to clean.

Self-Rimming (Rimless)

This lavatory has a lip that overlaps the cutout; it drops into a hole in the vanity top. Although it's easier to get behind the faucets to clean than with some other types, the joint line between lavatory and vanity top may be hard to clean. (See Figure 6–4.)

Undermounted

The lavatory overlaps the vanity top, but is secured with clips underneath. It is easy to keep clean except for the joint line between vanity and lavatory.

Integral

The vanity and the sink are one seamless construction that inserts into the vanity top. (See Figure 6–5.) It is very easy to keep clean, but if damaged both lavatory and vanity top will have to be replaced if they cannot be repaired.

Integral units of cultured marble can save you money. Instead of having to buy a lavatory and a countertop for, say, $150 and $50 each, the cultured marble unit is available for $150.

Solid-surface materials also come as integral units, and invisible repairs can be made. Prices can be reasonable: an integral Corian unit, for example, might cost only $50 more than buying a separate sink and countertop. Installation costs are about the same for integral units and for separate lavatories and countertops.

SIZES AND COLORS

Lavatories range from a tiny 12 by 12 in. up to sizes wide and deep enough to bathe a baby.

Figure 6–4.   Self-rimming lavatory. It is dropped into a hole in the countertop.

Figure 6-5. Integral lavatory. This one is made of reinforced acrylic. (Swanstone)

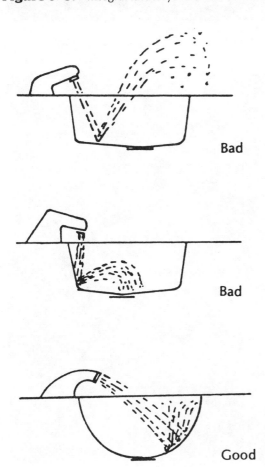

Figure 6-6. Good and bad faucet designs.

Normally, lavatories are mounted 32 in. off the floor (from the top of the lavatory to the floor), but some people who have studied it say that 34 to 38 in. is more comfortable because less bending is required.

Also, the water flow from most faucets usually does not extend far enough into the basin for easy hand washing. To make life easier, get a style that allows this. (See Figure 6-6.)

Like other fixtures, lavatories come in a wide variety of colors. The most popular color, according to the NKBA, is white—and it's also the least expensive.

FITTINGS

"Fittings" is really a technical name for faucets. They are available in a vast array of sizes, styles, and materials, ranging from the basic chrome-plated brass to those in the Vatican made of solid gold. (See Figures 6-7 through 6-10.)

Hot and cold water faucets come as one-piece units with projecting threaded shanks for insertion into holes in the lavatory or countertop. The distance between these holes is known as the faucet "center" (the center of

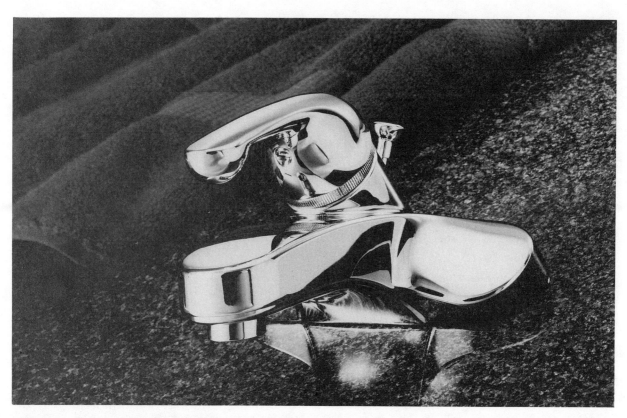

Figure 6–7. Single handle washerless lav faucet looks good and is not expensive. (Delta)

Figure 6–8. Faucets come in a large variety of sizes, shapes, and finishes. (Delta)

Figure 6-9. Victorian-style faucet from Epic is not necessarily better made than other brands; what you pay for is style.

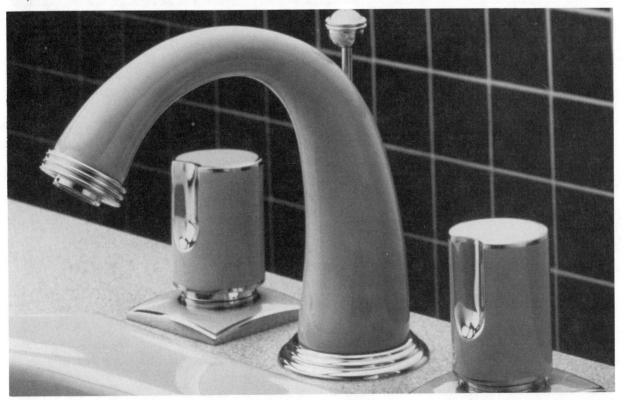

Figure 6-10. Here, again, faucets are well-made, but it's the style that will cost you several hundred dollars. They come in various hand painted colors. (Epic)

Figure 6–11. The closer the faucets are to one another, the harder they are to turn, as here. (T. Philbin III)

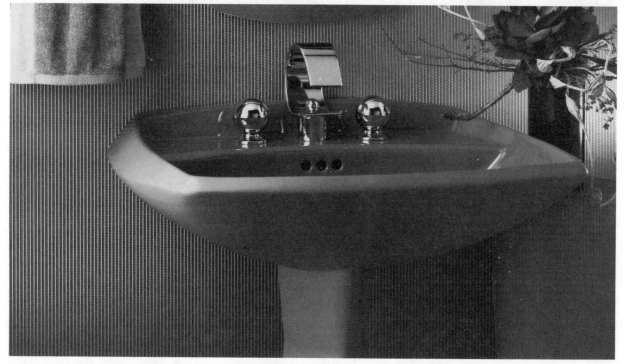

Figure 6–12. Faucets should not be shaped like these, which would be hard to grip with one's hands filled with soap. (Delta)

Figure 6–13. These faucet handles are easy to grip.

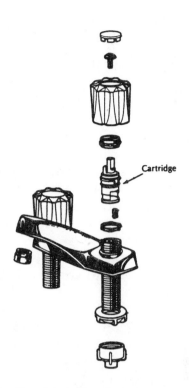

Cartridge

Figure 6–14. Washerless faucet.

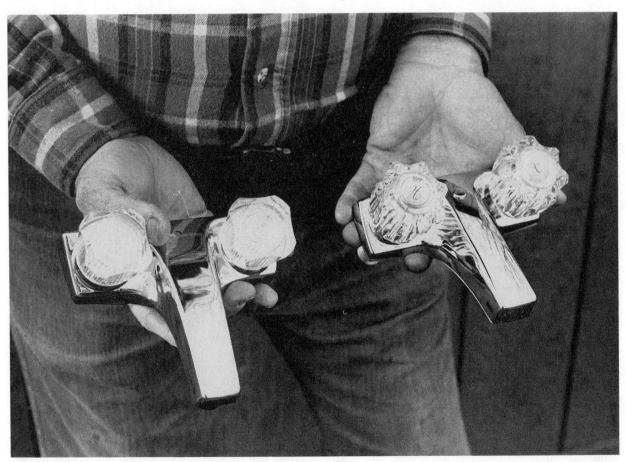

Figure 6–15. Heft faucets in your hand and you'll instantly see which manufacturer uses cast brass. (T. Philbin III)

the hot water handle to the center of the cold) and, of course, the faucet centers must correspond to the holes in the lavatory. Faucets for lavatories normally have 4-in. centers, but 8 in. is not uncommon, and you can get centers all the way up to 16 in. The rule is that the further apart the centers are (within reason), the easier the faucets are to turn and to clean (Figure 6–11). How many times, for example, have you stood in front of a lavatory and tried to manipulate too-close-together faucets with three or four fingers—particularly with fingers slick with soap and water?

The faucet handles should also be shaped so that they are easy to grip. If they're small and cylindrical, you're not going to be able to turn them as easily as if they were shaped like levers. (See Figures 6–12 and 6–13.) For the handicapped or elderly who have difficulty using their fingers, the single-lever faucets are best. Indeed, these can be operated by hand without required the use of individual fingers.

Many faucets are the so-called compression type. They work like this: You turn the faucet on and a threaded spindle with a soft washer on the end, which has been plugging up the hole or "seat" where the water emerges, comes out. When you turn the handle off, the spindle rotates down until the washer end plugs the hole again, turning the water off.

The other type of faucet is the so-called washerless type (Figure 6–14). The interior mechanism of this faucet has a disc cartridge, which is either ceramic or plastic. Ceramic is the better quality. Such faucets cost more than ones with washers, but they will last a lot longer and you won't have to change parts so often. They are more economical in the long run because you save on replacement parts and perhaps avoid a visit or two from the plumber. Also, the ceramic disc type is easy to repair: slip out the old disc unit and slip in the new.

FAUCET MATERIALS

Faucets are made of several different materials. Chrome-plated brass is the most common, but there are also chrome-plated plastic and plain plastic faucets. Chrome-plated plastic can be

good, depending on the brand you buy; pure plastic is not good. Chrome-plated brass may be tubular brass or solid brass. Solid brass is the best faucet you can buy. (See Figure 6–15.)

You can also get chrome-plated pot metal, but this is inferior. It pits and corrodes in no time. The problem is that chrome dresses up the pot metal to look like quality. To tell the difference between pot metal and solid brass, heft the pot metal in one hand, the solid brass in the other: the brass will be much heavier. Cast brass is also heavier than tubular brass. If you have doubts, ask the dealer.

MORE MONEY SAVERS

The happy fact about lavatories (as well as other fixtures) is that you can get a good-quality one inexpensively. The cost rises in relation to a lavatory's color and stylistic flourishes, not its intrinsic quality. So, for $125 you can buy a lavatory that has virtually the same quality as one for $700—the extra money is for color and style. The key is to buy only from brand-name manufacturers, such as Kohler, American Standard, or Eljer.

The same is true of fittings: the grander the style, the more you'll pay. But a cast brass faucet, even if it has little or no style, is still a quality faucet.

Another way to save is to buy your own fixtures. Years ago, this would have been difficult, but there has been a revolution in the business: plumbing supply houses, which used to sell only to plumbers, now will sell retail to anyone who comes in off the street. You can also buy direct from bathroom showrooms and home centers at big discounts.

First, visit a number of places to determine what you want, then start getting prices. You'll find that lavatory prices can differ as much as 30 percent and more. Simply get it at the cheapest price, then hire a plumber to install it.

One caveat: some plumbers who install your lavatory will not guarantee it against leaks and so forth. But a number of plumbers we spoke to said that if the lavatory has problems, it will have them right away—before the plumber leaves—so that he or she can fix it.

7

Toilets and Bidets

A toilet's basic flushing principle has not changed since it was invented over a hundred years ago in England by Sir Thomas Crapper. But there are still vast differences between today's toilets and the original water closet of Sir Thomas.

HOW TOILETS WORK

A toilet is a simple but ingenious device. All toilets work essentially the same way. (See Figure 7–1.) When the toilet lever is pushed, a certain volume of water—usually, 5 gallons—passes out of the tank and into the toilet, driving the existing water out of the bowl. As the tank empties a float ball inside goes down; the ball is attached to a rod, which is attached to a valve on a ballcock mechanism, allowing new water to flow in. As the water rises the ballcock mechanism is gradually turned off to stop the flow. There is also an overflow tube that shunts water into the bowl itself, filling it.

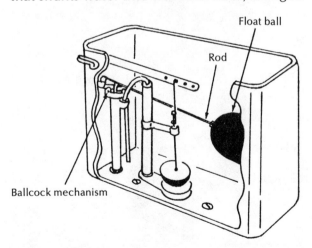

Figure 7–1. Mechanical innards of toilet tank. As the ball goes down, so does the water. As water goes up, the ball goes up and the end of the rod it's on turns off the ballcock mechanism, which is pumping water out.

As mentioned in Chapter 1, a crucial element of toilet design is the trap. This is a section of the toilet that is formed so that a certain volume of water is "trapped" in the bottom of the bowl after the flushing action is complete. This water acts as a seal against gases and vermin passing through the toilet and into the house.

DESIGNS

Toilets come in two basic designs: (1) close coupled, meaning that the water tank is a separate unit coupled or bolted to the bowl (Figure 7–2), and (2) one piece, in which the tank is part of the bowl design (Figure 7–3).

Toilets come with three different flushing actions: washdown, reverse trap, and siphon jet.

The washdown is used in other countries but no longer in the United States. It has the smallest water surface and the smallest trap opening—$1\frac{7}{8}$ in.—and is subject to fouling because the front area of the bowl is not covered with water and the small trap opening tends to clog. Both allow the bowl to become stained and contaminated easily.

The reverse trap has a larger water surface and a bigger trap; water enters the bowl through a series of holes on the underside of the rim. The result is minimal fouling.

The best design of all is the siphon jet (Figure 7–4). It has the biggest trap and the largest water surface, and the flushing action is the most thorough.

A good-quality toilet will have a good flushing mechanism. In higher quality toilets this mechanism is made of better materials and is more precisely engineered than are those for lesser toilets.

Figure 7-2. Two piece toilet—tank rides on back of bowl. Two-piece toilets cost less than one piece. (Eljer)

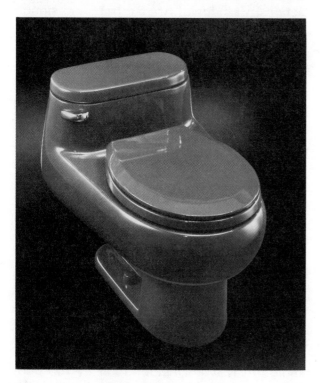

Figure 7-3. One-piece toilet. (Kohler)

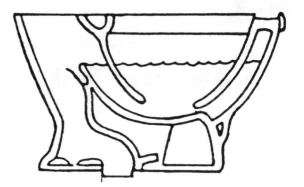

Figure 7-4. Interior of siphon jet bowl.

Another quality tip is surface finish. All toilets are made of "porcelain"—vitreous china. This is a hard, brittle material coated with a nonporous glaze. Better toilets—and this is obvious once you see them—will have smoother glazing and no pinholes in the glaze.

SPECIAL FEATURES

For years, standard toilets have used 5 gallons of water for flushing. Most manufacturers

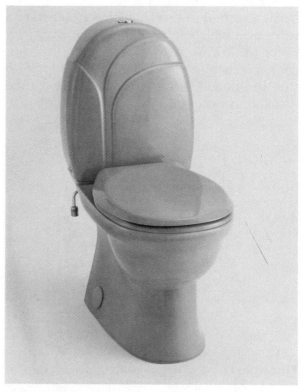

Figure 7-5. This two piece Eljer toilet uses only 3.5 gallons of water to flush.

today, however, make toilets that use only 3.5 or 1.5 gallons (Figures 7–5 and 7–6). Over a year, this difference can save significant amounts of water—and money. An average family using a 1.5-gallon toilet can save an astonishing 40,000 gallons of water a year. Today's units are much more reliable than the early water-saving models. These sometimes required several flushings to clear the bowl, thereby defeating the purpose of saving water.

It should be noted, though, that quality varies among water savers just as among standard toilets. Check the price—large differences are telling you something vital about what the manufacturer thinks of the product.

Toilets are also available with odor-eliminating features. Some work by creating a vacuum in the bowl; others require fans, complete with their own outlets.

Toilets are usually either round or elongated; elongated is more comfortable for men.

Toilets, like other fixtures, come in a wide variety of colors. Color costs more; you can save up to 25 percent if you are willing to use

white. (The vast majority of people do use white.)

No doubt the safest way to go when buying a toilet is stick to brand names: Eljer, Kohler, American Standard. Even though there are vast differences in price—$100 to even $900 within such brands, the quality differences are minimal; i.e., if you buy a $100 toilet in one of these brands it's not going to be vastly different from a $900 toilet. What will be vastly different is style. You will pay more for a siphon jet style than a close coupled style.

BIDETS

The bidet came into existence during Napoleon's time. Soldiers, used to riding horses all day, used to bathe their pelvic areas by sitting on a small carpenter's bench that in

Figure 7–6. This two piece toilet takes only 1.5 gallons. (Kohler)

Figure 7–7. Bidet. (Kohler)

French was called a bidet and in English means small horse. It was convenient and helped prevent irritations.

Eventually, the soldiers brought the bidet home and the entire family started to use it. Though not popular in America, it is widely used in Europe and is considered far superior to toilet paper. (See Figure 7–7.)

To use the bidet, a person completely disrobes and straddles the unit facing the faucets, which may be mounted on the bidet or in the wall. After use, the bidet is flushed.

The bidet is usually located right next to the toilet. Some bidets are linked to the toilet and feature hand sprays and/or air driers. Some do not require that the user disrobe completely. Some have seats, but most do not.

As with other toilets, bidets are mostly priced according to style.

UPFLUSHING

One other kind of toilet that's available can operate "below grade"—that is, below where it can be flushed normally, such as in the basement. This type flushes into a sort of holding tank, really a minicesspool, and then the waste is pumped up into a standard waste line, where it is discharged along with the rest of the waste flowing down the stack.

MORE WAYS TO SAVE

As with lavatories, it pays to shop around for toilets and bidets. First decide what make and model you want, then shop for the best price. Savings of 30 percent are not too much to expect.

Also, as mentioned in Chapter 1, it is cheaper to replace a two-piece toilet with a two-piece rather than a one-piece toilet (because then you won't have to lower the water line). If you live in an old house with a 10-in. or 14-in. rough-in for the waste pipe, it is much cheaper to find a toilet that fits than to use one of the more common toilets with a 12-in. rough-in—and have to move the waste pipe.

8

Tubs

In considering what tub to purchase, safety should be at least as important a consideration as comfort and style. According to many safety experts, the bathroom is the most dangerous room in the house, and the tub is the most dangerous single area. In an average year in the United States roughly 8,000 people fracture a bone, and 400 people die, as a result of accidental falls in the home, and the vast majority of these occur in the bathtub.

Like other fixtures, tubs are made of a variety of materials and in a variety of shapes and qualities.

MATERIALS

Cast Iron

Cast iron is generally considered to be the best material you can buy. Cast iron tubs are coated with a heavy layer of enamel. Because of its rigidity, cast iron resists chipping: when it is struck the coating does not flex and chip.

On the negative side, cast iron is extremely heavy—an average tub weighs around 500 pounds—and, as you might expect, it costs more than other types.

Enameled Steel

This is steel coated with enamel, though the coating is commonly thinner than that applied to cast iron. Steel tubs weigh about half what cast iron tubs do, but they are also noisier when water runs into them and will dent and chip much more easily. On the other hand, it is the least expensive tub of all, though the difference amounts to only about $100 per tub.

Fiberglass

Fiberglass tubs are available in a wide array of colors and shapes (more than other types). In addition, fiberglass is light. On the negative side, fiberglass scratches easily, but it can be easily spruced up with Soft Scrub.® (See Figure 8–1.)

Cultured Stone

These tubs are made of the same materials used to make lavatories and are part of the polyester family: material that is created by mixing any of various crushed stones—marble, onyx, or granite, for example—with polyester resin and then pouring it into a mold. Appearance varies depending on the stone used. For example, onyx creates a tub with a glassy appearance while granite looks freckled.

Like lavatories, cultured marble tubs have a gel coat that gives them their color and design. If this coating is chipped it can't be repaired successfully.

Cultured stone tubs are available in many colors, and they are easy to care for. They are far less expensive than tubs made of pure stone would be, but are not inexpensive. One of the great things about cultured stone, though, is that you can get all the fixtures with the same color and style. This isn't possible with any other material.

SHAPES

Tubs come in various shapes and constructions. The standard shape for a tub is rectangular, but there are also corner tubs with a round or oval bathing area. These tubs have

Figure 8-1. Fiberglass tub by Eljer.

two straight sides so the tub can be fit in a corner, and the front is a series of angles. Corner tubs are usually made of cast iron. (See Figure 8–2.)

Classically, tubs have only the front finished—or "skirted," as they say in the trade—but they are also available without a skirt, in case you are going to build a facing in front of the tub. Fiberglass whirlpools (see Chapter 9) can be bought with a removable skirting, a necessary feature for gaining access to and servicing the motor.

Generally, the tub sides are straight, but sloping sides and other configurations (such as armrests) may be part of the design.

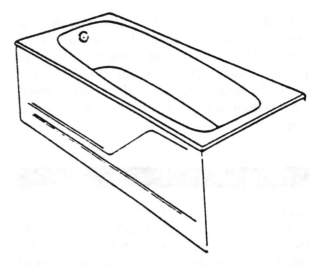

Figure 8–2. Classic tub with front skirted, sides missing.

Figure 8–3. Two-valve tub filler. (Peerless Faucet Co.)

Modern tubs usually have bottoms that are flush with the floor, but the old-fashioned clawfoot tub has enjoyed renewed popularity in recent years. This relic from the Victorian age has feet (actually feet and legs) that raise it off the floor; it is also known as a freestanding tub.

FITTINGS

A tub fitting or "faucet set" consists of either one faucet, with a single-handle valve for controlling both hot and cold water, or two valves, one for hot and the other for cold, and a spout (Figure 8–3). Technically, the former type is known as a one-valve tub filler; the twin-faucet fitting is called a two-valve tub filler. In the trade, tub fittings are also known as "brass" or trim.

Unlike lavatories, tub fittings have random centers—the distance between the centers of the hot and cold water handles. They may be 6 in., 8 in., 11 in.—whatever—because the centers are not critical for a successful installation. The faucet unit is connected to the water pipe and then the tile or wall material is cut to allow the faucet stems to poke through. With a lavatory, of course, the centers are important because the faucet water pipes must go through predrilled holes in the vanity top that are a certain distance apart.

In most cases, only the faucets are visible. Water pipes are hidden behind walls. With the clawfoot style, however, the water pipes are exposed and the centers on the faucets are usually 3½ in.

(Money-saving tip: If you are replacing a faucet and need to get to pipes concealed behind a tile wall, check to see if there is an open area or closet adjacent to or behind the faucets with a panel that gives access to them. Many times there will be, and even if there isn't you may only have to cut through

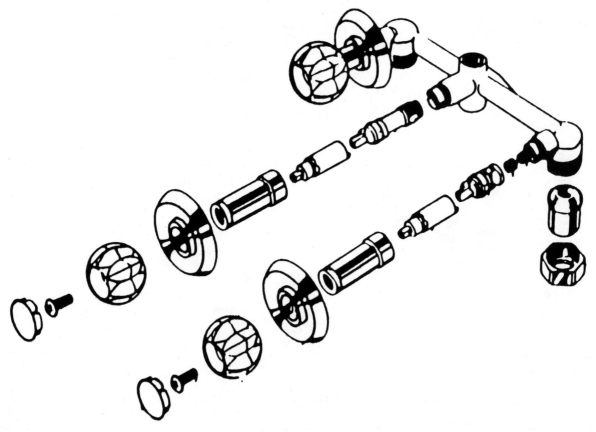

Figure 8–4. Exploded view of a three valve washerless bath faucet assembly. Diverter knob is in middle. (Peerless Faucet Co.)

Sheetrock to get to the pipes, a more desirable—and less expensive—alternative than breaking through ceramic tile.)

The faucet action may be compression or washerless (Figure 8–4). The former is less expensive but will require more maintenance (that is, replacing washers). Over time, the most economical way to go is to buy a washerless faucet. It uses a cartridge disc or ball instead of a washer. It lasts a long time, and when repair is needed it's easy to take the unit out and replace it.

QUALITY CRITERIA

The quality criteria for lavatory fittings also apply to tub fittings. In fact, tubs and lavatories are made of the same materials: cast brass, chrome-plated plastic, pot metal, tubular brass, and plastic. Cast brass is the best, chrome-plated plastic may be good, tubular brass is okay, pot metal and plastic are inferior. Your best bet is to stick with a brand

name and buy cast brass. But as has been said throughout this book, even brand name manufacturers make faucets of varying quality.

Drain mechanisms for a tub are purchased separately. There are two kinds: weight or piston type and spring type. (See Figure 8–5.)

The weight mechanism consists of a linkage connected to a weight that is lifted on and off the drain pipe by flipping a lever. This type of mechanism has no visible stopper.

The spring type also has a lever, but it is linked to a rocker-arm mechanism that operates a chrome stopper.

COMFORT AND SAFETY

While one presumably buys a tub to relax in, rather than just to clean one's body, the fact is that 90 percent of the time the tub is really bought as a shower (assuming you buy a standard size tub); a standard tub is simply not large enough to relax in. (See Figure 8–6.)

If you are thinking of the tub as a place to relax in, you should consider getting a separate shower and a larger tub. For example, standard rectangular tubs are 60 in. (5 ft) long, 14 to 16 in. deep, and 30 to 40 in. wide. A tub should allow you to stretch out full length and relax, so a 5-ft tub would be inadequate for a person who is, say, 5 ft 9 in. A heavyset person might find the 30-in. width constraining, and the 14-in. depth may be insufficient. Fortunately, larger sizes are available. In standard tubs, for example, lengths to 6 ft and depths to 20 in. can be purchased.

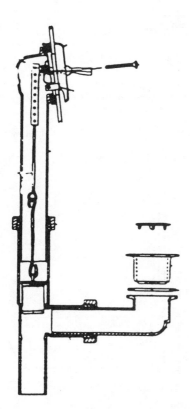

Figure 8–5. Polypropelene drain mechanism. This one is plastic, but they also come in brass which cost twice as much but are no better. (Peerless Faucet Co.)

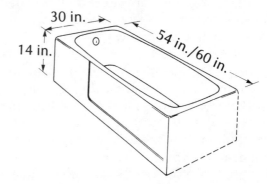

Figure 8–6. This is a standard-size tub—and at 5 ft long, it is too short for many people to relax in. You should be able to stretch out.

In some cases, there will not be room for a longer tub. But there may be room for one that's wider and deeper, and increasing these dimensions can add to comfort considerably. Square tubs are also available.

If you are going to be using a standard size tub, even a few inches can help. For example, New Canaan remodeler Mark Rutter commonly installs 60 × 32 × 16-in. tubs—and the extra space is significant.

INTERIOR SHAPE

Another comfort factor is the interior shape of the tub. Various companies make tubs with sloping sides, armrests, contoured bottoms, backrests, and more. A tub might seem, at first glance, as if it would be very comfortable. But listed overall sizes can be deceptive.

There is really only one way to find out if you'll be comfortable: try the tub out. Go to the showroom or supplier, take off your shoes, and sit in the tub. Showroom people are used to it. Indeed, they should encourage it. They want to sell you the unit that's right for you.

The same applies if a tub is planned for use by two people simultaneously. NKBA designer Ellen Cheever says that a tub for two people should be at least 42 in. wide. Here again, your best bet is to sit in the tub and decide if it's going to be comfortable or not.

(Incidentally, most water supply piping is ½ in., but if the tub is extra large—requiring more than 75 gallons of water to fill it—then make sure the pipe is large enough to maintain a steady hot water flow.)

One other comfort factor is easily accessible storage for shampoo, razor, sponge, and other items. This should be big enough to hold whatever you need and hidden from the view of anyone entering or just glancing into the bathroom. It is not difficult or expensive to build such storage units into the tub area, and there are also wire baskets that can be mounted on the wall itself. Wire baskets cost from $50 to $200.

SAFETY

As mentioned, the bathroom is a dangerous area of the home and the tub is the most hazardous part of it. To ensure the safety of anyone using the fixture, keep these safety factors in mind:

- The bottom of the tub should have a slip-resistant surface, or at least a slip-resistant mat. The bottom itself should be flat rather than contoured.
- Grab bars (preferably two) should be installed, ideally horizontally, where you can grab them to get in and out of the tub. (See Figure 8–7.) Any grab bar should be secured to the bath framing (studs) rather than the wall material and be able to withstand a pull of 300 pounds dead weight.

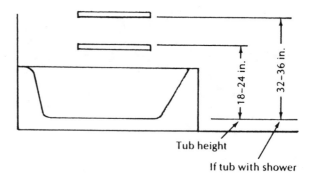

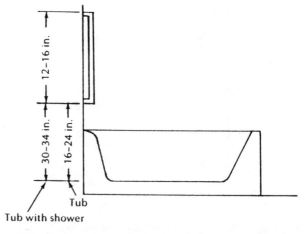

Figure 8–7. Good positions for grab bars.

Figure 8–8. For safety, you shouldn't have to reach far from tub for a towel.

- Soap dishes should be recessed—so they can't hurt anyone who falls—and can be reached easily. The same is true of wire baskets or other storage units.
- Towel rods or rings on the wall adjacent to the tub should be located so you don't have to stretch to get a towel.

- If the tub is sunken or is a platform type, you should be able to get in and out of it easily and grab bars should be installed where needed. (See Figure 8–8.) Steps should be large enough—at least 8 in. wide with a 7-in. riser (vertical portion).

MORE MONEY SAVERS

You can get a good-quality cast iron tub for a few hundred dollars; stick to brand names and you shouldn't go wrong. It makes little sense to buy a steel tub: it costs only an average of $100 less than cast iron but is more susceptible to chipping. In the long run you'll save money by going for quality.

As with lavatories and toilets, price differences will reflect color and style rather than quality—as long as you stick to brand names.

As with other fixtures, shop around. Home centers, showrooms, and—increasingly— plumbing supply outlets will sell directly to homeowners. Once you visit these places and decide what you want, buy the least expensive fixture and hire a plumber to install it. Some plumbers will not guarantee the installation but most will.

9

Whirlpool Tubs

Many people get confused about the differences between a whirlpool bath, a hot tub, and a spa. A whirlpool bath is simply a tub that has ports from which jetted water issues, powered by a pump. It takes the place of a conventional bathtub and is emptied after each use, like a regular tub. The theory is that moving water is more relaxing than still water.

A spa is shaped like a whirlpool but is not drained after each use. Rather, it heats, filters, and recirculates the same chemically treated water for two or three months. Whirlpools are permanent installations, built into an enclosure or tiled into a tub surround and requiring installation of water lines, faucets, and drain line. Spas, on the other hand, are available as in ground or portable units that do not require special plumbing—a garden hose will work fine. Generally, whirlpools are designed for one or two people, while spas usually seat two or more.

A hot tub is simply a large wooden tub capable of seating several people. A heater maintains constant water temperature, but there are no jets. Hot tubs are the forerunners of today's spas, although relatively few of them are manufactured now.

IS A WHIRLPOOL FOR YOU?

A whirlpool tub is not essential, so before deciding to install one, you should consider a number of issues. How badly do you want the comfort of a whirlpool? Realistically, how frequently would you use it? Can you see yourself sitting in one reading a book at the end of a long day? Would the kids want to join you?

Another question is affordability. Whirlpools generally begin at about $1,000 and can cost up to $5,000. (Details on cost are included at the end of the chapter.)

WILL IT FIT?

Whirlpools come in a variety of shapes and sizes and will fit in most homes. You can get them in the same standard size—5 ft long by 32 in. wide—that bathtubs come in; in that case they'll fit into a standard bathtub alcove (Figure 9–1). Some models are as small as 4 ft long, and some are shaped to fit into corners.

If you have the space—and the money—you can also get larger models—5½ or 6 ft long and 36, 42, or 48 in. wide—and bigger.

INSTALLATION

Most whirlpool baths are designed for either recessed or drop-in installation.

Recessed whirlpools will fit into the usual bathtub alcove. Such whirlpools have either a nonremovable apron or one that can be removed to provide access to the pump and motor that power it. If you wish, the removable apron can be replaced with tile, mirrors, wood, or whatever suits the design.

A drop-in whirlpool comes with a "rolled" rim and may or may not have an apron (Figure 9–2). This type is set in the floor or in a raised platform, installed in a conventional alcove, or located with one or two sides adjoining a wall. Most installations will require a crawl space (below the floor) to drop the tub into.

Faucets and spouts for the whirlpool may be mounted on a wall, on the deck surrounding the whirlpool, or on the whirlpool itself.

Figure 9–1.   Some whirlpools will fit into the same size alcove that a standard tub will. (Kohler)

Size and Weight

If the whirlpool is larger than average, consider whether or not it can be physically moved through the house for installation. Sometimes it simply can't be done. Tricky, tight turns in halls or stairways could sabotage your installation plans.

Although the weight of the whirlpool is less likely to be a problem than most people realize, you will want want to make sure that its weight can be supported wherever it will be installed. Typically, a whirlpool will weigh about 50 pounds more than a regular tub of the same dimensions. If the whirlpool's dimensions are larger, so much the better: the weight is spread over a larger area of the floor, resulting in better support. One installer said that a group of people standing around at a cocktail party would create a heavier load on a floor than would a whirlpool with water and one bather.

Platform Type

If the whirlpool is to be mounted in a platform, there should be space around it for one or two 8- to 12-in.-wide steps—the length of a person's foot. The edge of the whirlpool should be 4 in. to no more than 12 in. from the edge of the platform, for easy access. Bathers should be able to sit on the platform edge and swing their legs into the water. Floor surface, steps, and platform should be made of slip-resistant material, such as textured or unglazed tile. The whirlpool itself should have a slip-resistant bottom or tape. (See Figure 9–3.)

Figure 9–2. Whirlpool with apron. There should be easy access to the motor. (American Standard)

Electricity and Plumbing

If the whirlpool is to be installed on the second floor and there are no water supply or drain lines there, make sure that lines can be brought down through walls or, more cheaply, through closets.

For safety, whirlpools should be on dedicated circuits. A 115-volt line will usually maintain water temperature or even raise it by a few degrees. It is more energy efficient to maintain warm water temperature than to constantly run cold water until it becomes warm.

A whirlpool must have a GFCI (ground fault current interrupter) for safety.

The whirlpool pump and motor must be accessible for servicing. A typical solution is to locate the whirlpool so that there is access through a closet or cabinet on the other side of the wall.

Ventilation is also necessary, but this can usually be handled by an ordinary exhaust fan.

WHIRLPOOL MATERIALS

Like other fixtures, whirlpools come in a variety of materials.

Cast iron coated with enamel is generally considered the best material you can buy. With care, it will retain its high gloss for decades. (See Figure 9–4.)

Cast acrylic is much lighter than cast iron and is available in more different shapes.

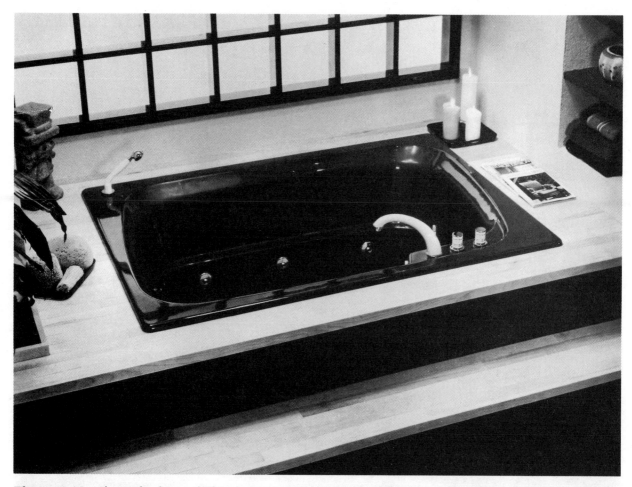

Figure 9–3. If steps lead to a whirlpool, they must be sized for safety 8-in. to 12-in. wide. (American Standard)

Figure 9–4. Cast acrylic whirlpool. Because it is light and easy to work with, it is often used for tubs (as here) that can accommodate more than two people. (Eljer)

Because of its light weight, it is often used for larger pools.

Fiberglass coated with a gel is not as thick as acrylic sheet, but it can be easily repaired if damaged.

Cultured marble is plastic manufactured to look like marble.

Enameled steel is at the low end of the quality scale. It looks good but is susceptible to chipping and rusting.

OTHER CONSIDERATIONS

You should consider comfort when selecting a whirlpool. As with a tub, you should fit into it comfortably; the best advice is to sit in it to try it out.

The water jets should rotate easily. Jets that are difficult to move make it harder to get the desired massage action. You might want to get separate controls for air and water at each jet to customize the flow.

The on/off switch can be a wall-mounted type which requires the bather to get out of the bath to turn it off or one that's mounted on the bath, readily accessible.

A good feature to look for is a safety shutoff that will turn the whirlpool off after a specified time so it doesn't run on its own if left unattended; the shutoff also serves as a reminder of bathing time. Some newer whirlpools have a shutoff that activates if an intake is blocked.

The pipes underneath the whirlpool should be copper or rigid polyvinyl chloride (PVC),

Figure 9-5. The pipes on a whirlpool should be rigid PVC or copper, not flexible PVC. (Eljer)

not flexible PVC (Figure 9–5). Flexible PVC can sag over time; when water collects and bacteria breed there, a foul odor or even a health hazard can result.

The whirlpool should carry a Underwriters Laboratories (UL) seal for the entire whirlpool, not just the components (such as the pump). This ensures electrical safety.

COST DETAILS

As mentioned earlier, whirlpools start at about $1,000 and can cost more than $5,000 for very large models or those made from specialty materials, such as teakwood.

A bath-mounted on/off control will cost more than a wall-mounted switch.

A heater will add about $400 to the cost.

Faucets and other fittings must be purchased separately. Prices start at around $150 and go to $800. (For more cost details, see Chapter 12.)

To all this, you must add the cost of installation of electrical and plumbing work.

The whirlpool should also come with a warranty.

SAVING MONEY

You can save money on a whirlpool the same way you can on any other fixture: find out what brand and model you want, then shop around for the best price—there can be a 30 percent difference.

It is a good idea to stick to brand names—Kohler, Eljer, or American Standard. Different types of whirlpools will have different quality characteristics, but all major brands within a type will be equally good. For example, if you buy a steel tub you'll get a lesser tub than if you bought cast iron, but at least with a brand name item you'll get something that's as good as possible given the material.

10

Showers

There are a variety of different shower types, from tub/shower combinations to freestanding, self-contained units.

FAUCETS

For tub/shower combinations, the fittings either may be separate hardware or may be used to control both shower and tub by means of a diverter, a valve that lets you switch between shower and faucet. Four faucet arrangements are used: the three-valve diverter, the two-valve diverter, the two-valve shower fitting, and the single-valve diverter.

The three-valve diverter consists of hot and cold water faucets that control both shower and tub (Figure 10–1). If you turn the diverter knob one way, the water is routed into the tub; if you turn it the other way, the water comes out of the showerhead.

The two-valve diverter consists of hot and cold water faucets and a pop-up diverter (stopper) on the tub spout. Pushing the stopper down directs the water to the tub; pulling it up routes the water to the showerhead.

The two-valve shower fitting consists of hot and cold water faucets for the shower only, with no connection to the tub; the tub has its own faucets.

The single-valve diverter is connected to both the tub and the shower. It is pressure sensitive and ensures that water flowing from either the shower or the tub has a constant temperature. (More details are included in the section on safety and comfort later in this chapter.)

HEAD SEPARATE FROM FITTINGS

The showerhead is separate from the faucet fittings. It may come either with or without a pipe on it. It is secured to a supply pipe that extends up from the faucets.

Unlike lavatory valves, which have specific centers, shower valves have random centers.

The same quality criteria as used for lavatory or tub fittings also apply to shower faucets. Cast brass is best, tubular brass is okay, chrome-covered plastic can be okay, and plain plastic and pot metal are inferior.

SHOWERHEADS

Like faucets, showerheads come in varying degrees of quality and in a few different styles.

The older type consists of an adjustable showerhead attached to an arm, which is then connected to the water pipe. To replace the head, the arm is either unscrewed or unsweated (a torch flame is applied to melt the solder used to join the arm to the head) (Figure 10–2).

The newer heads are simply unscrewed from the end of the pipe projecting from the wall.

Hand-held showerheads secured to a flexible line are also available. Their big advantage is that you can control the water stream completely, keeping your hair dry if you wish. The composition of the water stream can also be controlled, from pulsating to what is known as "champagne"—air mixed with water.

Figure 10–1. Three-valve diverter. (Eljer)

Figure 10-2. Unscrewable shower arm.

(Money-saving tip: Shower hardware can be replaced. Since changing faucets buried in a tile wall can be expensive, check to see if there is a panel behind the wall, or close to it, that will give access to the faucets. If not, there is usually a closet behind the fittings. In this case, you can cut through what is likely to be a Sheetrock wall. This is far easier, neater, and cheaper than cutting through a bathroom wall covered with tile.)

ONE-PIECE SHOWERS

Freestanding, one-piece showers are strictly for new work, simply because they are too big to fit through doorways in existing houses. You can, however, get prefabricated three-piece showers that can be assembled in the bathroom.

A one-piece shower comes with sides but may or may not have a drain pan or top. Such showers are commonly made of plastic-reinforced fiberglass, but you can also get enameled steel or enameled tin. The best showers are fiberglass, and they come in a variety of colors (Figures 10-3 and 10-4). Enameled steel and tin come only in white. They are noisy and susceptible to chipping and consequent rust. Steel is better than tin.

PANS

Separate shower pans or bases are available for use with one-piece or custom-built showers. Pans come in three standard shapes: square, rectangular, or angled to fit into a corner. They are made of molded stone, terrazo,

or acrylic. They have a 2-in. drain hole and are usually 5 to 6 in. deep.

You can also make a custom pan by building a wood framework, setting the pan in place, and then installing tile or other water-resistant material over it.

TUB SURROUNDS

Tub surrounds come in either fiberglass or plastic and consist of three or five walls, each made to fit into one of the walls in the standard tub alcove (Figure 10-5). They are designed for use with standard-size tubs and save money because they replace tile, which would cost more because installing it is more labor intensive. (See Figure 10-6.)

Holes may be drilled through the walls for tub and shower fittings. Some walls come with predrilled holes for the fittings to be slipped through.

SHOWER DOORS

Shower doors come separately from the shower itself; they consist of the door and a framework.

Doors are designed for installation in various situations and may be hinged, folding, pivot, or sliding (Figure 10-7). They have a metal frame and may be aluminum- or brass-colored.

For safety, the glass used must be either tempered or laminated plastic. The glass or plastic comes in a limited number of colors. It is also possible, however, to get laminated glass etched shallowly or deeply with designs; this is relatively inexpensive.

Shower doors also come with mirrored glass, a boon if you want to make the room seem larger.

SAFETY AND COMFORT

The shower is one area where much can—and should—be done to ensure the comfort and safety of the user.

Figure 10-3. Fiberglass shower, the best kind you can get. (Eljer)

Figure 10–4. Tub surround made of reinforced acrylic. (Swanstone)

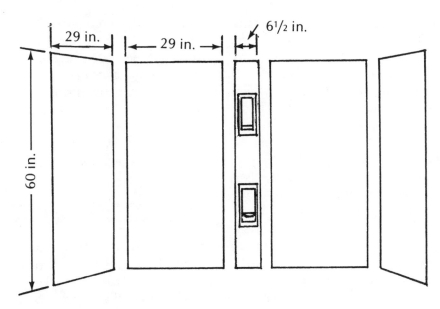

Figure 10–5. Five parts of tub surround.

Figure 10–6.   Shower surrounds are also sold in one piece. (Swanstone)

Consider the fittings. If the water pressure is erratic, the hot and cold water flow can also be erratic. For example, if someone is standing under a shower and a toilet is flushed elsewhere in the house, the cold water flow is instantly reduced, resulting in the person getting scalded—or possibly more seriously injured when he or she spontaneously jumps to avoid the sudden stream of very hot water.

There are a number of specialized fittings that mitigate this problem, and one of the best, if not *the* best, is the pressure-control valve (Figure 10–8). These valves contain innards that automatically sense when water pressure is imbalanced and compensate instantly. For example, if a toilet were flushed, the valve would immediately reduce hot water flow so that the ratio of hot water to cold would stay constant—and the user would not get scalded.

Such valves come with mechanical innards made of plastic or ceramic. Ceramic is better. The Symmons Company of Braintree, Massachusetts, makes an excellent unit that can be

installed new or added during remodeling. Thus, an ordinary valve can be changed to a pressure-balancing type without having to break up the wall. The adjacent photos show how it's done.

Another good comfort and safety feature in a one-piece shower is a seat (Figure 10–9). Sitting down while shaving your face or legs is a lot safer than standing.

Also, if the shower does not have a nonskid surface, get a mat or use abrasive tape to make it nonskid.

Extra-wide showers are also available for the handicapped. (See Figure 10–10.)

SAVING MONEY

The classic way to save money with showers is to install a reduced-flow showerhead. Showers normally use around 6 to 8 gallons of water per minute, but there are some reduced-flow heads that cut the flow to below 3 gallons

Figure 10–7. Hinged doors. They come separate from the shower, like regular doors. (Eljer)

Figure 10-8.   This type of faucet guards against one being scalded—or frozen—when taking a shower. (Symmons)

Figure 10-9.   A seat is very good to have in a shower. Sitting is more convenient when shaving your legs, for example. (Corian)

per minute. As designer Ellen Cheever points out in her book *The Basics of Bathroom Design . . . And Beyond,* using reduced-flow showerheads "can save the average family of four as much as 36,500 gallons of water annually, based on a daily five minute shower per person."

In addition, she points out, you will save the costs of heating some of that water. But she adds that such heads may not be cost-effective in areas where the water is soft and the flow is light: this can translate into longer showers to rinse soap from hair, for example—defeating the water-saving purpose.

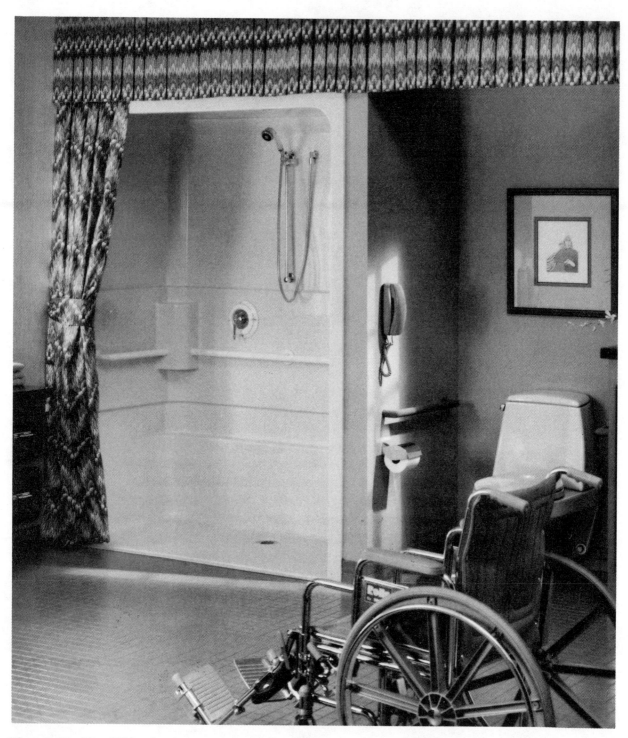

Figure 10–10. Wider shower surrounds are also available for use by the handicapped. (Kohler)

11

Fixture Layout

Whenever new fixtures are installed, you should observe certain principles to make the fixtures easier to use and to promote safety. Each fixture requires a certain amount of space around it to be used conveniently. If the spaces are too small, the fixtures can be difficult and uncomfortable to use.

Following is information on minimum and liberal clearances.

TOILET AND BIDET

The minimum clearance for toilets is at least 2 in. from the side edges of the bowl to any obstructions, such as walls. The following clearances are better:

- If the toilet is between two fixtures, it should be set in a space 30 to 32 in. wide.
- If the toilet is between two walls, the space should be 30 to 44 in. wide.
- If it is between a fixture and another wall, the space should be 30 to 36 in. wide.

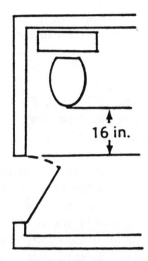

Figure 11–2. There should be at least 16 in. of space between the end of the toilet and the door opening.

If a bidet is used by itself, it should be set in a space at least 36 in. wide. If used with a toilet, there should be between 30 and 44 in. between the center of each fixture.

Toilets and bidets also require sufficient knee clearance, which ranges from 21 to 30 in. (Figure 11–1). If the toilet (or bidet) is directly in front of a swinging door, there should be at least 16 in. of space so that if the door is opened it will not strike anyone using either of the fixtures. (See Figure 11–2.)

LAVATORY LAYOUTS

The big space needed here is *between the vanity cabinet* the lavatory is set in (or, if it is a pedestal lavatory in which no vanity is used, between its edge) and any wall or fixture opposite it (Figure 11–3). Anywhere from 21 to 30 in. is adequate for another person to pass through.

In some cases, where there is a separate tub, it will be set next to a lavatory. Here,

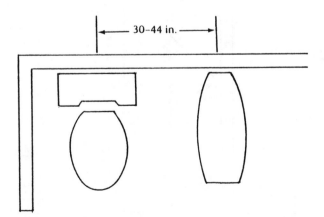

Figure 11–1. Toilet and bidet should be 30 to 44 in. apart.

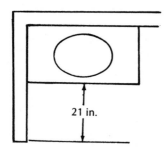

Figure 11–3. Minimum space between wall and lavatory is 21 in., 30 in. is much better.

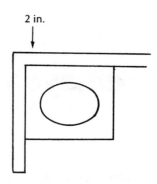

Figure 11–5. The vanity should have at least 2 in. of space between the end of the bowl and the adjacent wall.

there should be at least half a foot of space between them so that the sides of the shower and vanity can be easily cleaned (Figure 11–4).

Another desirable layout feature is enough room on the vanity top to set various articles such as shaving gear when the lavatory is being used. No lavatory should have less than 2 ft of wall space. If the vanity is set in a corner, there should be sufficient room between the edge of the lavatory and the wall: 2 in. is minimum, 6 in. is better. (See Figure 11–5.) If there is a double lavatory, there should be at least 4 to 11 in. between the two.

In a large bathroom, where space is not at a premium, it does not matter whether a person is left- or right-handed: generous amounts of space can be provided on both sides of the lavatory. In a small bathroom, however, it usually does matter, and if you have to make a choice it's better to have most of the space to the right of the lavatory if the user is right-

handed, and most on the left if he or she is left-handed.

SHOWER AND TUB CLEARANCES

There should also be adequate clearances between the tub and shower and the wall or fixture opposite them. Include 21 to 30 in. of clearance between the tub and shower and the wall or fixture (Figure 11–6). Note that some shower doors are wider than 21 in.; the clearance should be great enough that the door, whatever its size, can clear it.

Finally, there should be at least 2 ft of towel hanging space for each person who uses the bathroom.

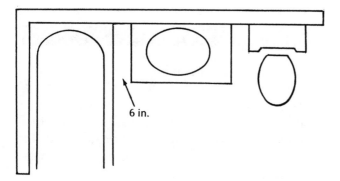

Figure 11–4. There should be 6 in. of space, to facilitate cleaning, between the lavatory and other fixtures.

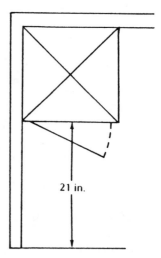

Figure 11–6. The shower should have a minimum of 21 in. of space between it and the wall.

Costs

12

There are two kinds of costs involved in installing bathroom fixtures: (1) costs for simply replacing fixtures, not disturbing the existing plumbing, and (2) costs for new work, where new water and waste lines must be installed in addition to the fixtures.

LAVATORIES

Remove and replace existing wall-hung lavatory with 20 × 18-in. wall-hung lavatory. (Lavatory: $80; faucet: $50; trap assembly: $30): $484.50

New work: $1,056.00

Replace 20 × 18-in. lavatory set in cultured marble top on prefinished cabinet base. (Lavatory: $50; trap assembly: $30) The costs of vanities (21-in. deep) and tops would be as follows:

Vanity Width (in.)	Vanity	Plus Top
24	$225.00	$ 757.50
30	$285.00	$ 862.50
36	$345.00	$ 967.50
42	$405.00	$1,072.50
48	$465.00	$1,177.50
60	$585.00	$1,372.50
New work:		
24	$225.00	$1,329.00
30	$285.00	$1,434.00
36	$345.00	$1,539.00
42	$405.00	$1,644.00
48	$465.00	$1,749.00
60	$585.00	$1,944.00

Replace pedestal lavatory with pedestal lavatory. (Lavatory: $220; faucet: $50; trap assembly: $30): $787.50

New work: $1,056.00

TOILETS AND BIDETS

Replace existing toilet with two-piece, floor-mounted toilet. (Toilet: $105; seat: $20; water supply: $20): $375.00

New work: $1,497.00

Replace one-piece toilet. (Toilet: $305; seat: $25; water supply: $20): $757.50

New work: $1,879.50

Replace floor-mounted bidet. (Bidet: $200; brass fittings: $350): $1,350.00

New work: $1,836.00

STANDARD/WHIRLPOOL TUBS

Replace existing standard tub with 5-ft tub. (Faucet: $60; drain assembly: $75) The total costs would vary, depending on tub material, as follows:

Cast iron ($250):	$1,252.50
Steel ($150):	952.50
Fiberglass ($170):	1,057.50
New work:	
Cast iron:	$1,716.00
Steel:	1,416.00
Fiberglass:	1,521.00

Replace whirlpool tub, 5 ft long by 30 in. wide by 18 in. deep. (Three jets including skirt: $1,580) (Note: cost of electrical work and ceramic tile not included.): $3,150.00

New work: $3,975.00

EXTRA COSTS FOR COLOR

As noted in the text, color costs more. To the fixture prices above, add the following costs if the fixtures are a color other than white.

Lavatory:	$ 42.00
Two-piece toilet:	37.50
One-piece toilet:	102.00
Standard tub:	121.50
Bidet:	181.50

SHOWERS AND TUB ENCLOSURES

Replace existing defective shower pan (after wall, pan, and floor tile have already been removed) and install new shower pan: $850.50

Install neo angle shower enclosure with 24-in.-wide side panels, 27-in. door, 72 in. high, smoked glass.

New work: $360.00

Install tub wall kit—three vinyl wall sections.

Economy grade:	$156.00
Medium:	261.00
Premium:	486.00

Install fiberglass shower stall, including rough plumbing.

New work: $897.00

Install fiberglass tub/shower unit, including rough plumbing.

New work: $1,645.50

Install folding doors with aluminum frame, plastic panels, fold 12 in. for up to 66-in. opening, 58 in. high: $241.50

Install bypass doors, two plastic panels, aluminum frame, in opening 58 in. high and up to 60 in. wide: $208.50

Tempered glass: $262.50

Install hinged door with aluminum frame, with tempered glass door in 48-in. opening: $253.00

CABINETS AND STORAGE

If you are saddled with a small bathroom, there are limits to what you can do to improve it. Nonetheless, one thing you can do—and it will improve the bathroom light years—is to increase storage facilities. Most small bathrooms—indeed, most bathrooms—suffer from a severe shortage of storage. This certainly needn't be so. This section contains a roundup of what's available in cabinetry, as well as some storage ideas that will show you how to make better use of what you have.

Cabinets

13

Bathroom cabinets come in a variety of different styles and sizes, but usually are made either of wood or of wood products covered with plastic laminate. Most cabinets are basic vanity types, but some have special features and variations. For example, you can get tall cabinets, cabinets with pull-out hampers, cabinets with drawers, and very

---

Vanity Tops

Vanity tops come in various styles and sizes.

One type is plywood covered with plastic laminate—Formica. On this type you make a cutout for the lavatory, which is then dropped into the vanity cabinet. Plastic laminate is available in a wide array of colors and styles and is the cheapest top available. It comes in high-pressure and low-pressure grades. Low pressure material is "soft" and should be avoided: it won't stand up well to wear and tear.

Another type is the integral top, made of a solid-surface material, such as cultured marble, reinforced acrylic, or—very popular—Corian®, a hard plasticlike material that looks good and wears very well. These tops incorporate the lavatory and the rest of the top in one molded piece. Many designers prefer such tops because they're easy to keep clean—no seams.

Another type of vanity top is covered with ceramic tile. A plywood panel is cut, the cutout for the lavatory is made, and then the tile is adhered to the top. You can use oak or metal edging to dress up such a top, giving it a little more pizazz than plain tile edging.

When buying any top, make sure it has enough room on the sides to lay grooming aids.

---

narrow cabinets. With luck, such units will fit your situation exactly.

Cabinets may also be purchased with various finishes and different handles, knobs, and so forth, which can help the cabinet fit better in your design scheme.

Cabinets come in two styles: classic American "face frame" or European "frameless." Face-frame cabinets have a frame front into which the door closes; frameless or overlay types do not. Face frame looks better in conventional bathrooms. Frameless has a distinctively modern look. (See Figures 13–1 and 13–2.)

You can get both wood and laminate-covered cabinets in three basic forms: stock, semicustom and custom.

STOCK CABINETS

Stock cabinets come in a series of set widths and heights; they are sold in lumberyards, home centers, and cabinet shops. (See Figure 13–3.)

Stock vanity cabinets are available from about 2 ft to 6 ft wide. Heights may be anywhere from 30 to 36 in. Such cabinets either come with a cutout for a sink or have no top and are designed to accept an integral lavatory plus top (Figure 13–4).

Of the three forms of cabinets, stock are the least costly, but they have a major disadvantage: they come only in set sizes. If you happen to have an odd-sized space to fill, you can't use a bigger cabinet, and using a smaller one robs you of storage space. For example, if your space were 27 in. wide and the closest size you could get were 24 in., you'd have to fill the extra 3 in. with a filler

Figure 13–1. European style cabinet. (Crystal Cabinet Works, Inc.)

Figure 13-2. Face frame cabinet. Face frame is used more often for conventional settings, European for modernistic. (Quaker Maid)

Figure 13–3.   Most wood cabinets (80%) are made of oak, such as here. (Mannington)

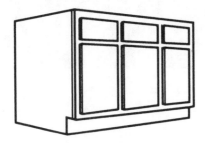

Figure 13–4.   Basic vanity cabinet. It comes without a top.

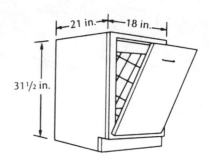

Figure 13–5.   Hamper cabinet.

board, thus losing valuable storage space. (See Figures 13–5 through 13–8.)

SEMICUSTOM CABINETS

These cabinets come in a much wider variety of sizes than stock cabinets. Manufacturers keep cabinet parts in the factory and list the cabinet sizes available in their catalogs. You select the size and style of cabinets you want and order them. The cabinets are assembled at the factory and shipped to you.

A variation is cabinets built on the job site. The carpenter will build cabinets to fit your space using stock cabinets and filler boards.

CUSTOM CABINETS

For custom cabinets, you go to a cabinet shop and tell the cabinetmaker what sizes you need; he or she then builds them to your exact specifications.

The big advantage of custom cabinets, in the words of bathroom specialist Mark Rutter, is that "you are able to use every single inch of space that's available." With stock cabinets this is usually not true; semicustom cabinets are better but not as space efficient. Custom cabinets also offer a wider choice of woods and finishes: the limit is what you have to spend. Custom cabinets tend to be wood, and oak is far and away—well over 80 percent—the most popular wood used.

QUALITY CONSIDERATIONS

Cabinets may be built of either wood or laminate-covered wood products. They come in varying degrees of quality.

There are several ways to tell if a wood cabinet is of high quality. The best way to learn about cabinets is to visit outlets that sell them (home centers, plumbing supply houses, even kitchen cabinet showrooms that often also sell bathroom cabinets, and ceramic tile showrooms). Look inside and outside the cabinets—and at the back. Low-quality cabinets

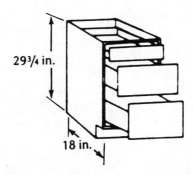

Figure 13–6. Three-drawer vanity. Drawers can be handy for organizing things.

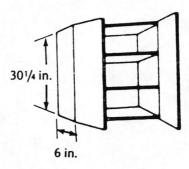

Figure 13–7. The cabinet shown here is designed to be hung on the wall.

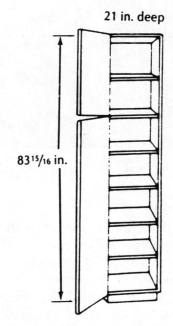

Figure 13–8. Tall cabinet. These are very efficient storage units because they use a lot of otherwise empty wall space.

Figure 13–9. Medicine chests can be surface mounted or recessed, as shown here. (Quaker Maid)

look and feel flimsy; they may have been whacked together with staples. Good-quality wood cabinets are solid and well constructed. The wood part is usually thicker and the joints are better, dovetail (like fingers interwoven), mortise and tenon (a tongue fits into a slot) instead of butt.

Also, look at the hardware—the hinges and handles. Does it seem substantial and

solid? After you've looked at good hardware and bad hardware, the differences should be apparent.

Another quality check is to try the doors and drawers. Do they slide or open easily and solidly? On drawers, check the slide mechanisms. Are they solid metal track with ball bearings, or a hunk of wood screwed to the side that rides in a slot?

Wood cabinets come with a clear coating, usually lacquer, but this does not relate to quality.

Good-quality plastic laminate cabinets are covered with high-pressure (as opposed to low-pressure) laminate. High-pressure laminate is thicker and harder—it will stand up much better to scrapes and dings than will low-pressure material. Ask the salesperson what it is.

Again, examine the cabinets as you would the wood types. Quality will shine through.

MEDICINE CHESTS

Medicine chests are available in two basic styles: those designed for installation between studs (14½ in. wide), and those that are meant to be surface mounted (Figure 13–9).

You can get them with single or double mirrors or with triple hinged mirrors that can be turned for the most advantageous viewing.

SAVING MONEY

One good way to save on cabinets is to buy stock—they cost only half what custom units cost. You'll have to be lucky, though, to have cabinet size correspond with the space available. Your chances are increased greatly if you use modular cabinets, simply because there is a greater range of sizes available. Happily, these cabinets do not cost a great deal more than stock sizes, because manufacturers are set up to produce them almost like stock.

Plastic-laminate-covered units are cheaper than wood.

14

Storage Principles

As you create storage space in the bathroom, there are a number of principles you should try to follow to ensure maximum use from the storage units available.

First, make often-used items easy to get at (Figure 14-1). For example, makeup and shaving gear should be right near the vanity, and you shouldn't have to reach or bend too much to get them. The ideal height for such items is between 22 and 56 in.

Store things that are not used often in the more out-of-the-way spots (Figure 14-2). For example, if you have a foot-soaking device, you could store it on top of a unit that hangs on the wall above the toilet.

Another good idea is to store like items together (Figure 14-3). For example, store shaving gear and aids together; store makeup items together; and store toothpaste, dental floss, and so on together.

Narrow shelves work better than deep ones—things can get buried in deep shelves and will be hard to get at. (See Figure 14-4.)

SAFETY

As with other areas in the bathroom, safety is a prime concern. Following are some safety tips.

- If a cabinet is installed on the wall above the toilet, it should be no more than 8 in. deep so that someone rising from the toilet won't hit his or her head.
- Any area containing supplies potentially hazardous to children should have a lock.

- Cabinets should be planned so that doors do not open into passageways.
- Vanities should have a kick space of at least 3 x 3 in.
- Hardware used on drawers should be smooth and designed so that it would be difficult for it to catch on clothing and pull the drawers out.

STORAGE IDEAS

Here are some storage ideas that you can adopt, or adapt for your own use.

- Built-ins. Storage units can be mounted between studs by removing wall material, a simple job. Such storage is particularly desirable in a small bathroom—the less the storage juts into available space, the better. The wall depth is usually only about 3 in. or so, but the square footage adds up. (See Figures 14-4 through 14-6.)
- There's no reason that cabinets can't be mounted above the mirror, space that is often unused.
- The wall above the toilet is an obvious place to mount a storage unit but it's often overlooked. Indeed, think of all wall space as potential storage.
- Raise the vanity and install drawers. Many vanities can be raised and drawers installed under them.
- Use tall cabinets. Ones that go from the floor to the ceiling will allow that much more storage space. If space is at a premium, use narrow, shallow cabinets.
- Use open shelves for easy access to items (Figure 14-7).

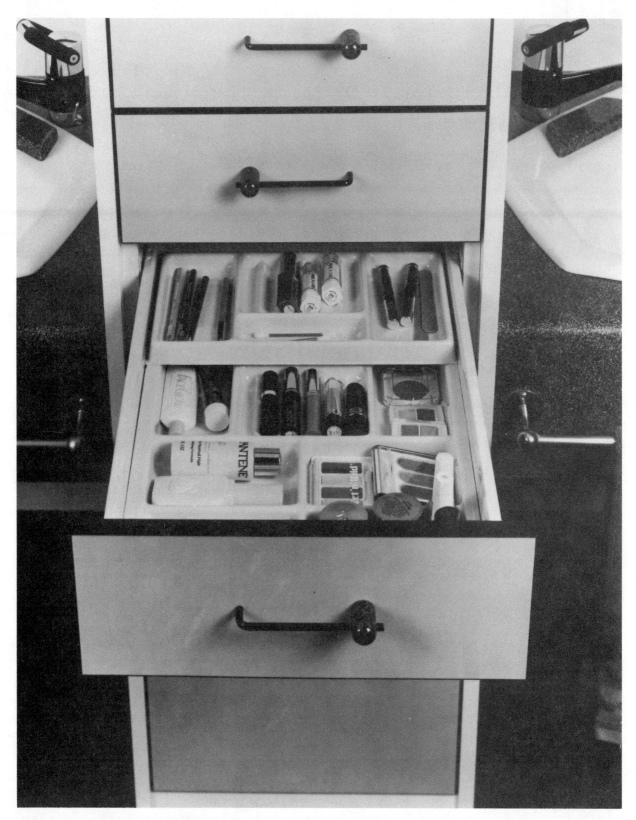

Figure 14–1. Often-used bathroom items should be easy to get at. These cosmetics are in a compartmentalized cabinet drawer between dual vanities. (Wood-Mode Cabinetry)

Figure 14-2.   Things you don't use much can be stored high up. (Crystal Cabinet Works, Inc.)

Figure 14–3. Like items should be stored together. (Quaker Maid)

Figure 14–4. A built-in magazine rack by the toilet is a good idea.

Figure 14–5.   Here, the enameled door of a medicine chest has been covered with wall covering. (Nutone)

Figure 14–6. Space between studs represents new storage galore for most bathrooms. Visualize all empty space as potential storage space. (Nutone)

Figure 14–7.   Compact cabinets have open shelves for easy access to items. (Kemper)

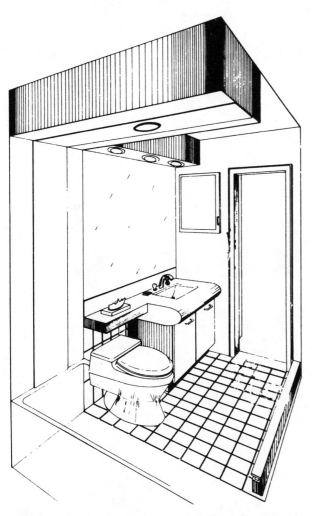

Figure 14–8. Banjo vanity. It is built so that part of it extends over the back of the toilet, creating additional storage space.

- Have a "banjo" vanity built. The vanity can be built so that part of it extends over the toilet tank. (See Figure 14–8.)
- If you have enough space, install a pullout hamper. It's very convenient to have one in the bathroom.
- Install the medicine chest on a wall adjacent to the vanity, and put a big mirror over the vanity. The medicine chest can be as large as you like as long as it does not seem oversized for the room.
- Install the vanity in an adjacent bedroom, and use the extra space created for more storage.

Part 4

HEAT, LIGHT, AND VENTILATION

Three areas where many bathrooms fall short are heat, light, and ventilation. All, of course, are very important and are not difficult or very expensive to improve.

15

Heat

Many people shiver when they contemplate an early winter-morning trip to the tub or shower. They know that before the bathroom warms up they're going to be cold. Such discomfort isn't necessary. There are a number of different ways to make sure the bathroom is warm before you arrive.

NEW BATHROOM

If you're installing a new bathroom, you might be able to extend the heating system you already have. Even if you're not building a new bathroom, you may be able to use the existing system.

The two basic kinds of systems are hot air and hot water. In the hot-air type, air is heated by a furnace and then routed through ducting to emerge at hot-air registers.

In hot-water systems, water is heated in a boiler, and then the hot water is carried through pipes to radiators or heat registers where it gives up its heat. The cooled water recirculates back to the furnace where it is heated again and begins its journey back to the radiators or registers.

A QUESTION OF EXPENSE

Whether or not you can extend your existing system depends on capacity and cost. First, the heating system must have the capacity to provide the heat for the extra bathroom. Chances are, it will.

Another important consideration is how expensive it will be to extend the system. It is usually fairly cheap to extend a hot-air system: you just extend ducting so that it vents into the bathroom. Using the flexible ducting that is now available makes this job even cheaper than it used to be.

Hot-water systems may be more problematic and costly because you have to extend plumbing—hot water pipes—and you may also need a new radiator or baseboard heating registers.

If new capacity is needed, this does not mean that you need a new furnace. You may be able to modify the existing furnace, such as by increasing the size of a feeder nozzle on an oil burner or increasing the jet sizes on a gas unit. A bigger pump may spirit the water along more efficiently, or you may need a new fan if an added volume of hot air is being routed through ducting.

In any case, these are questions that a heating specialist should answer. Generally, heating the entire space of an average-sized bathroom will require an additional 1,500 watts of power. If extending the system is impractical, a number of separate heating sources may be more practical—and cheaper.

SEPARATE HEAT SOURCES

Following is a list of separate heat sources and what they can—and cannot—do. All are electric.

- A wall heater should be on its own dedicated 220-volt circuit. It has its own thermostat, so it turns on and off independently of the house heating system. Such heaters will heat an entire bathroom. (See Figure 15–1.)
- A toe-kick heater is installed off to one side in the toe-kick space of the vanity, rather than in the center (Figure 15–2).

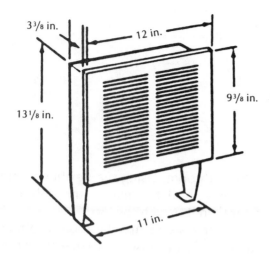

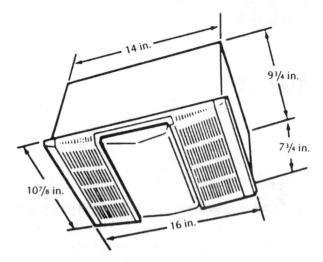

Figure 15–1. Wall heater. It has a 1500-watt capacity, adequate for heating most bathrooms.

Figure 15–3. Heater/light combo. The heat produced is usually not sufficient to warm the entire bathroom. (Nutone)

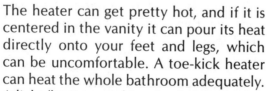

Figure 15–2. A toe-kick heater warms the floor well. (Nutone)

The heater can get pretty hot, and if it is centered in the vanity it can pour its heat directly onto your feet and legs, which can be uncomfortable. A toe-kick heater can heat the whole bathroom adequately.

• A light/heater combination is mounted in a ceiling and furnishes light as well as heat (Figure 15–3). It can increase the air temperature a bit, but it won't heat the entire bathroom as much as some people like. Such combination devices do not need separate electrical circuits.

Figure 15–4. Radiant heat will warm the bathroom completely. Cables are laid, then cement poured. (Thermafloor)

- Radiant heat is perhaps the most desirable auxiliary heating system of all (Figure 15-4). It consists of electric coils that are laid on the floor and then covered with cement. The result is a warm bathroom floor, and the heat radiating from the floor fills the room. Consider radiant heat if you are planning a new floor.

For safety, no matter how chilly a bathroom gets, you should never use a portable heater. Electricity is in close contact with water, and that's a potentially disastrous combination.

SAVING MONEY

The key way to save money is to carefully consider all the options detailed above and then select the one that's cheapest for you while fully satisfying your heating needs.

16

Lighting

Proper lighting in a bathroom is far more important than most people realize, for at least three reasons. First, there is simply the matter of seeing oneself better. It can be frustrating to try to shave or apply makeup with inadequate lighting. Second, different lighting will show color in different ways. A pink vanity, for example, will look substantially different when lit by different kinds of light. And third, lighting affects mood. Going into a bathroom lit with harsh fluorescents, with all the ambiance of the local police station, can be a disconcerting, uncomfortable experience.

BULBS

There are two kinds of bulbs: incandescent and fluorescent. Both types are rated by wattage: the higher the wattage, the brighter the bulb.

Incandescent bulbs have a filament wire that is heated until it glows, emitting light. Fluorescents are filled with an inert gas and coated with phosphors. When electricity flows into the tube, the phosphors absorb energy and emit light.

Incandescent bulbs, which can be obtained in a variety of shapes, emit a warm, soft light that is easy on the eyes and flattering to skin. Fluorescents give a colder light that is generally harsher on skin, although some are available that emit light similar to that of incandescents.

Fluorescents are usually considered to be much more cost effective than incandescents, generally providing twice the light for the same power. Because fluorescents take a lot of energy to start, however, they may not be so efficient in the bathroom, where the light may be switched on and off frequently.

GENERAL AND TASK LIGHTING

Rooms are illuminated by two kinds of lights: general and task. General lighting refers to a light that illuminates the entire room. The fixture may be mounted on the wall or on the ceiling. Task lighting provides light to a specific area, such as a vanity.

To determine how much light a room should have, lighting engineers suggest the following rules of thumb. If the general lighting fixture is in the open rather than recessed, it should provide $1/2$ watt of light for every square foot in the bathroom if it is incandescent; if it is fluorescent, $1/3$ to $1/2$ watt is adequate, because fluorescents provide more light per watt than do incandescents. If the general light fixture is recessed—in a high hat (a canlike fixture "buried" in the wall or ceiling) or the like—more wattage is required: $2 1/2$ to 4 watts per square foot for incandescents and $1/2$ watt per square foot for fluorescents. These values apply in a room with light colors, where light reflectance is good. In a dark room, more light would be needed.

A dimmer switch, which controls the light level, is a bright idea.

HALOGEN LIGHTS

Halogen lights, which have long been used only commercially, have made some inroads into private bathrooms in recent years. These lights come in a variety of shapes and sizes and emit a warm but very bright light that makes glass glitter and adds a lot to the appearance of a bathroom, while providing good illumination.

Halogen lights use low voltage and come with a transformer that reduces the regular line voltage in the house.

VANITY LIGHTING

The most important task lighting area in a bathroom is the vanity, because it is here that grooming takes place. A vanity should be a light color, which reflects the light well.

There are three kinds of vanity task lighting: above the mirror, theatrical (around the mirror), and on the sides. (See Figures 16–1 and 16–2.)

Incandescents of 60 to 100 watts are favored for above mirror lighting. The fixture

Figure 16–2. Task lighting may also be mounted on the sides of the mirror. (Nutone)

should provide even light along the entire mirror and be mounted 78 in. above the floor. Additional fixtures should also provide even illumination along the sides. Such fixtures can use bulbs mounted 30 in. apart and 5 ft high (from the center of the bulb to the floor).

Theatrical lighting runs up the sides and across the top of the mirror. The top of the fixture should be 78 in. off the floor. One caveat: If you live in a warm area, you may want to avoid using theatrical lights, because they generate a lot of heat. If you do use them, a dimmer switch is a good idea.

(Incidentally, a bathroom mirror should not be veined; this type doesn't reflect light well enough.)

OTHER TASK LIGHTING

If your bathroom is compartmentalized, task lighting can work well in the various areas.

The tub area is a good example. Many men shave in the tub, and an extra light may be

Figure 16–1. Vanity lighting is classical task lighting. The medicine chest comes with lights built in. (Nutone)

Figure 16–3.   Recessed light is good for providing light in the shower. (Corian)

necessary. A 60- or 75-watt recessed vapor-proof incandescent bulb is ideal (Figure 16–3). Some codes, however, prohibit lighting above a whirlpool tub because it is considered a pool, and no light is allowed above a pool. Check your local building code. A dimmer switch works nicely here to reduce light levels when you want a certain ambiance while bathing (Figure 16–4). Any fixture for the tub area should have its switch mounted where it cannot be reached from the tub or shower—to prevent a serious shock.

Use a *20-watt fluorescent* tube or a 75- to 100-watt incandescent wall or ceiling fixture to provide reading light for a compartmentalized toilet area.

Some people have enough space in the bathroom to create a laundry center. In this case, use a task light mounted about 4 ft above the washer and dryer. For ironing, you can mount adjustable lights with 150-watt reflectors on the ceiling a couple of feet in front of the ironing board.

Figure 16–4. A dimmer lets you lower the light, creating a certain ambiance. (Kohler)

SAVING MONEY

Fixtures come in a tremendous array of styles and prices. One way to save is to simply shop around. Fixtures often carry a 100 percent markup. Ask for 40 or 50 percent off.

Another way to save money is to use just general lighting rather than task lighting, or use just vanity lighting for the entire bathroom. Your decision depends on how big the bathroom is and how much light you want or need beyond the basic wattages recommended at the beginning of this chapter.

Sometimes just increasing the size of a fixture can give you all the light you need and eliminate the expense of other fixtures. For example, one designer told me that instead of a 2-ft fixture over a 4-ft-wide vanity, he installed a 4-ft fixture; it provided all the light needed for the entire room.

Skylights

Skylights have become very popular in recent years, and it's easy to see why. For one thing, they can flood a room with light. For another, they can help with energy bills, providing solar heat in the winter. They can be good for ventilation in any room in the house, but particularly in the bathroom, where an open skylight can bleed off potentially harmful moisture-laden air (Figure 17–1). Indeed, energy technicians say that as long as skylights don't comprise more than 10 percent of a roof's area, they will be energy efficient. Skylights also provide a glare-free, diffused light that is excellent and shows the true colors in the bathroom.

More than all this, skylights are simply nice, and by letting part of the sky into a room they make the occupants feel more expansive.

MATERIALS

Skylights are available in two materials: glass and plastic (acrylic). Glass skylights are always flat, while plastic skylights always have a dome shape (indeed, the basic idea for their design came from the plastic pods used in flying fortress aircrafts). (See Figure 17–2 and Figure 17–3.)

Plastic

Acrylic skylights come with either a single dome or a double dome made of a two-layer sandwich of plastic. The double-dome air space may be sealed or unsealed. Unsealed double domes should be avoided because moisture can get in and condense.

Acrylic skylights come in a variety of colors. The most common is clear, but translucent white, bronze, and gray are also available.

Clear acrylic skylights allow more than 90 percent of the light to pass through them, and you should carefully consider this fact before purchasing one: that is a lot of light, glare, and heat from the sun. Perhaps the best bet is to find a house with a skylight and see it in place.

Translucent white allows in only about 50 percent of the light, while gray and bronze allow in half that. Double domes are available with combinations of colors—for example, bronze outside layer and clear inner layer.

Glass

As mentioned, glass skylights are always flat. The glass should be tempered. Glass that is not tempered could be a disaster waiting to happen.

Today you have a choice of plain or "low-E"—for "low-emissivity"—glass, which means that the glass is impregnated with a virtually transparent metallic material that lowers energy costs.

FEATURES

Skylights are either fixed or movable. In fixed skylights, the glass or plastic either cannot be opened or can be opened only manually with a pole. A movable skylight is one operated by an electrical motor. Such skylights are also known as roof windows.

Skylights are available with a variety of other features, including shades and blinds.

109

Figure 17–1. Skylights can help rid the bathroom of excess humidity. (Ventarama Skylight Corp.)

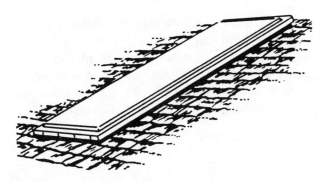

Figure 17-2. Glass skylights are always flat.

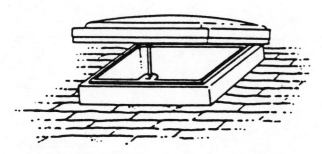

Figure 17-3. Acrylic skylights are always dome shaped.

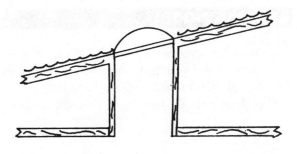

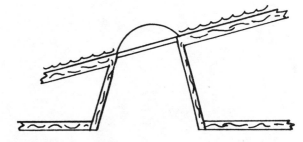

Figure 17-4. Light shaft. A flared shaft costs about 40 percent more than a straight one.

SIZES

Skylights come in a variety of sizes, many designed to fit between existing rafters, spaced either 16 in. apart or 24 in. apart. To save money it's always a good idea to get a size that will not involve cutting into the rafters.

The average bathroom will not need more than one skylight: it is estimated that one square foot of skylight can light 20 square feet of area.

INSTALLATION

If you buy a good quality skylight, you will not have to worry about it leaking. It won't. The problem with skylight leakage—and it is a big problem—is improper installation. As someone once said, "You can't fool the water." If there's an opening the water will find it—though maybe not right away. Leaks can show up long after the installer has left. For example, falling leaves may form a dam around the skylight, and standing water will then find its way into an opening that it might not have entered if it were just running down the roof rapidly during a rainstorm.

Installers say that the older the roof, the more likely the new skylight is to leak. Debate exists as to what the best installation methods are.

In some cases, it will be possible to install a skylight in the roof directly above a bathroom, but it is more likely that a light shaft will have to be built (Figure 17-4). Here, the skylight is installed in the roof, and then a Sheetrock shaft is built with an opening made in the ceiling.

QUALITY

Skylight quality varies. Because there are many different factors to consider, we recommend that you buy by brand name. Four good brands are Venterama, InsulaDome, Wasco Industries, and Velux.

SAVING MONEY

One way to save on an acrylic skylight is to buy only the insulated, double-dome type. The double dome will reduce heat loss much better than a single-thickness skylight will.

Low-E glass skylights, which are designed to conserve heat, are a good buy. One industry insider predicts that in the future all glass skylights, as well as windows, will use low-E glass.

Also, shop around for skylights. Prices on the same skylights can vary 25 percent.

18

Ventilation

A bathroom ventilating system is important for removing odors, but it is even more critical for controlling moisture. Uncontrolled moisture can destroy bathroom materials—loosen wall-covering seams, rust fixtures, break down paint, and so on.

It is obvious that bathroom activities generate a lot of moisture, but it might be good to understand why. The problem is not just the moisture itself, but the fact that the bathroom is warm. Warm air can hold much more moisture than cold air, resulting in high humidity, a measure of how much moisture the air can hold at a particular temperature. The higher the temperature, the more moisture the air can hold, and the higher the humidity will be. Compare, for example, the high humidity at the equator and the low humidity in Antarctica, which is virtually *all* water (sea and ice). Antarctica is much less humid because the cold air doesn't hold the moisture as well.

The real culprit in the bathroom is condensation: when the warm, moist air contacts a relatively cool surface, the result is condensation: the surface sweats. You can see the condensation on surfaces such as a toilet or medicine chest mirror.

Figure 18-1. An exhaust fan is designed to be mounted in the ceiling. It is available in various sizes to handle bathrooms up to 85 sq ft. (Nutone)

temperature in the bathroom too rapidly, causing the user to be chilled. The idea is to remove the air quickly enough to prevent condensation, while still allowing the room to stay comfortable.

The Home Ventilating Institute suggests using a fan that can change the air in the room eight times per hour. Air exchange is measured in CFM (cubic feet per minute), and the CFM will be marked on the fan.

The formula for getting the CFM needed is as follows. Multiple 1.7 times the area of the bathroom and round it off. For example, a 5 x 7-ft bathroom would be 35 square feet times 1.7, or 59.7. Round this off to get 60 CFM. (Note: the calculation assumes an 8-ft ceiling.)

REMOVE MOISTURE . . . BUT NOT TOO FAST

A variety of exhaust fans are available to remove moisture-laden air and odors. Some are just fans, some are a combination of fans and lights, and some have fans, lights, and heaters built in. (See Figures 18–1 through 18–4.) A key consideration is not to remove the air too quickly. Doing so can reduce the

NOISE

Exhaust fans are constructed differently: some have centrifugal blades instead of impeller

Figure 18–2. This unit could serve as a general lighting fixture for the bathroom. It takes a 100-watt incandescent bulb (a hinged lens swings down so you can change the bulb) and is rated at 2.5 sones. (Nutone)

Figure 18–4. This is a concealed intake exhaust fan. The fan is covered by a hinged door that can be painted or papered to match the decor. Open the door to use the fan, close it when not in use. (Nutone)

Figure 18–3. It looks like just a light, but it's also a fan. This handsome oak-stained ceiling unit projects only 1⅝ in. from the ceiling when installed. The manufacturer says it shouldn't be installed directly above a shower or tub. (Nutone)

blades; some are insulated; some are mounted on rubber; some are beefy enough to resist vibration, and some are relatively flimsy. These factors all contribute to the noise the fan makes when running, and this is measured in sones. One sone is about equal to the amount of noise a running refrigerator makes.

Fans are rated on a scale of 1 to 10. Most pros recommend that a bath fan should not exceed 3 sones. Such fans are not the cheapest, but neither are they exorbitantly expensive. You can get fans as low as 1.5 sones (they remove 90 CFM), 2.5 sones (130 CFM), and 3 sones (150 CFM). The sone level will be imprinted on the fan.

Figure 18–5.   A movable skylight can also be helpful in removing humid air. (Wasco Products)

OPERATING DIFFERENCES

A fan may be operated like a light switch—you turn it off and on—but a variety of fans with automatic controls are also available.

One type is a unit in which the light and the fan go on and off at the same time. This prevents the user from forgetting to turn the fan on or off.

Another type has a dehumidistat. The fan's operation is tied to the level of humidity: when the humidity increases, the fan goes on; when the humidity decreases, the fan goes off. This type is particularly good where children, who are apt to forget, use the bathroom frequently.

Another type of exhaust fan has a timer. When the fan is turned on, the timer keeps it running for a specified period of time.

WALL OR CEILING MOUNT?

Exhaust fans are designed to be mounted in either the wall or the ceiling.

It is usually easier to mount the fan in an exterior wall. Just cut a hole, insert the fan, and that's about it.

A ceiling unit requires duct work to route the hot air into the great outdoors, and this is, of course, more difficult and expensive.

"It's also better," says Mark Rutter, head of Projects Plus, a New Canaan, Connecticut, firm. He explains: "Hot air rises, and more of it gets to the ceiling than to a side wall. There's simply a more direct route for the hot air to travel to the outside."

Rutter says that routing the fan duct to the roof is usually the cheapest way to go, but since there is a fan hood outside, says Rutter with a chuckle, "It sounds like it's raining in the bath."

OTHER VENTILATING IDEAS

Another good idea for ventilation is to have adequate space under the door. If the door is flush with the threshold, moisture-laden air is blocked off.

A skylight can also help to bleed off moisture-laden air (Figure 18–5). Following use of the bathroom, the skylight can be cracked open; the warm, humid air will bleed out quickly. The skylight can be manually opened with a pole or, preferably, operated by a switch control.

Finally, there are toilets that have built-in controls for eliminating odors (see Chapter 7).

19

Costs

LIGHT FIXTURES

Ceiling fixture with switch.

New work where framing is
open: $108.00
Old work—wire fished up through
walls: $141.00

Fluorescent fixture over medicine cabinet, one tube and one plug, including outlet, fixture, and switch: $262.50

Recessed 12 × 12-in. fixture, including fixture, outlet, and switch.

New work: $178.50
Fished: $327.00

WALL FANS

Install exhaust fan: $225.00

Install 1000-watt combination
heater: $267.00

Install combination fan, heater, and
light: $325.50

DUCT WORK

Metal duct work for fan installation
without breaking through a wall: $17.00/ft

Break through wall and vent fan.
Frame (wood) wall: $42.00
Masonry wall: $76.50

Vent fan through roof of single-story
house: $69.00

CEILING FANS

Install ceiling fan using existing
wiring: $213.00

SKYLIGHTS

Install fixed skylight in fiberglass or asphalt roof. Job includes installing headers in rafters, a 2 × 6 wood curb, patching roof as needed, finishing interior with unfinished wood trim. Skylight is wood, double-glazed tempered glass, frame clad with aluminum.

Frame Dimensions
22 × 30 in.:	$ 846.00
22 × 45½ in.:	933.00
30 × 22 in.:	846.00
30 × 30 in.:	900.00
30 × 45½ in.:	1023.00
45½ × 30 in.:	1023.00
45½ × 45½ in.:	1166.00

Ventilating (Movable) Skylight

Outside Frame
22 × 30 in.:	$ 909.00
22 × 45½ in.:	1007.00
30 × 22 in.:	909.00
30 × 30 in.:	965.00
30 × 45½ in.:	1107.00
45½ × 30 in.:	1107.00
45½ × 45½ in.:	1260.00

If skylight is installed in roof with roofing other than asphalt or fiberglass, add the following:

Built-up:	$375.00
Slate:	325.00
Cedar shakes and shingles:	150.00
Spanish or mission tile:	350.00
Concrete roofing tiles:	300.00

Skylight Accessories

Rod control for blinds or windows:	$ 60.00
Electric window motor control:	320.00

Light Shafts

Build light shaft from rafters to flat ceiling below, including installing headers on existing ceiling joists, framing out shaft from existing headers to new joist headers, and installing drywall and taping (no painting).

Up to 2-ft shaft:	$320.00
2 to 4 ft:	452.00
4 to 6 ft:	574.00
6 to 8 ft:	696.00
8 to 10 ft:	816.00

If the shaft is flared, add 40 percent to prices.

BATHROOM ACCESSORIES

Accessories are a small but vital part of bathroom design. A touch here and there can mean a lot in a bathroom and, happily, the average person can apply those touches. The following chapter gives information on what's available and some tips on using it.

20

Accessories

There was a time not too long ago when bathroom accessories were very limited—perhaps a few towel bars, a soap dish, a toilet-paper holder, a toothbrush and tumbler holder. Such accessories might be available in white vitreous china or polished chrome, and that would be about it. This is emphatically no longer true. Today, people see the bathroom as a place where good design belongs, and this includes paying attention to details. Details, as it happens, can make a big difference in the overall appearance of the bathroom.

VARIETY OF STYLES, COLORS

There are many different styles and colors of accessories. It is easy to match the color and style of fixtures, thereby creating a unified

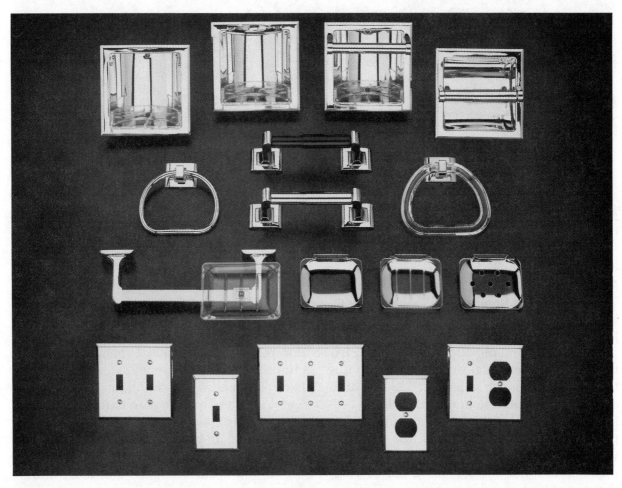

Figure 20–1. Having accessories with the same look can go a long way toward unifying the bathroom design. (Nutone)

Figure 20–2. When buying fixtures, buy from the same manufacturer to insure the same colors. Accessories can then be bought to blend in with fixtures. (Eljer)

look in the bathroom (Figure 20–1). For example, if you want faucets with a brushed-chrome finish, look also for brushed-chrome towel bars and a toilet-tissue holder in a complementary style.

The same principle applies to colored fixtures, fittings, and accessories. Although it is not possible to get a perfect color match among the various elements, you will do better if you stay within one manufacturer's product line (Figure 20–2). If, for example, you use the fixtures and fittings of one manufacturer and the accessories of another, the chance of matching colors perfectly is slim.

Perfection also will not be possible in terms of the finish on various colored items. If you have almond faucets, almond fixtures, and an almond countertop or wall material, the finishes on the various surfaces will be different, no matter what manufacturer you choose. Faucets may have a wet-paint look, fixtures made of china will have a subdued-wet look, and plastic laminate will have a dullish finish, while ceramic tile walls will have a shine, but it will not match the gloss of other surfaces.

Still, finish doesn't make that much difference, and close colors will tend to blend together. Of course, you couldn't have a bone white and a gray white together and expect them to blend.

OTHER ACCESSORIES

Towel bars, tumbler/toothbrush holders, and soap holders, may be considered standard accessories, but there are other accessories that can help carry out the design theme in a room. Examples: towel rings, mirrors, shelves, robe hooks, wire baskets, cabinet knobs, and toilet trip levers. (See Figures 20–3 and 20–4.) If these fit the overall design, they help to reinforce the theme.

Sometimes it won't take much to create a theme. "For example," says Doris Nardelli, accessories specialist for the Kohler Company, "antique-style faucets and accessories, paired with a mirror in an heirloom frame, can suggest a period motif without a major redo." And, she adds: "Accessories are small items that allow the consumer to be the designer. They offer a lot of opportunity for individual expression." (See Figure 20–5.)

MIRRORS

Mirrors are one of the more important accessories in the bathroom. They are, of course, functional, but their design value as shall be detailed below can also be extremely important.

The mirror may or may not be part of a medicine chest. They come in a variety of shapes and styles as well as colors—some have designs etched on the face, others are plain. Frames vary greatly too, from traditional polished chrome to oak (Figure 20–6). Mirrors without frames are also available. Some mirrors are multiparted and angled so that they can be manipulated and brought closer to the face.

Another extremely handy mirror is one that mounts on a wall and can be pulled out for use with scissorslike collapsible legs. This is handy when two people are using the bathroom at the same time: one may be using the medicine chest mirror, while the other can pull out the other mirror for shaving.

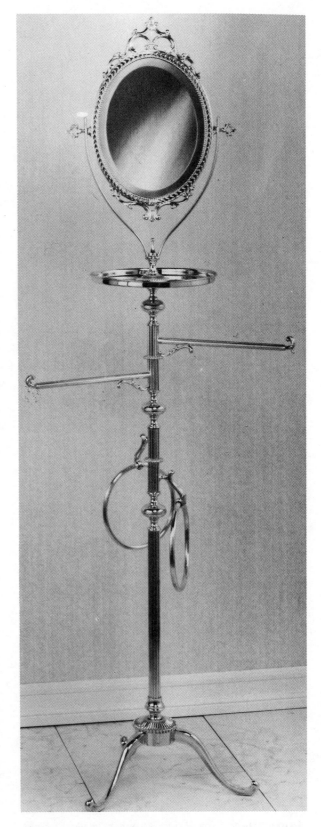

Figure 20–3. Freestanding towel rack. If you like the antique look in a bathroom, it fits well. (American Standard)

Figure 20–4. Towel ring. (Eisenhart Wallcoverings)

Figure 20–5.   Here, ladder for hanging towels fits into modernistic design quite nicely. (Mannington)

Figure 20–6. The wood-framed mirror shown also comes with matching light fixtures. (Kemper Cabinets)

Figure 20–7. Sheet mirrors are not expensive but can visually expand the bathroom. Of course, the mirror uses potential storage space, which may be the top priority. (American Standard)

Mirrors can visually increase the size of a room. For example, installing floor-to-ceiling mirrors can make the room appear higher; a mirror can be placed on one end of a room to widen it. (See Figure 20–7.)

Floor-to-ceiling mirrors can be individual units or sheets. Sheets work quite well. Call a local glass company and order what you want and they will install it for you.

Sheet goods are not expensive. For example, if you got a 4 × 4-ft sheet of mirror, it might cost you $160 plus $90 for installation, for a total of $250—not a lot of money in relation to the outstanding design help it gives.

GRAB BARS

While grab bars may not be glamorous, they certainly rate high in the safety department—yet many bathrooms are not equipped with them. (See Figure 20–8.)

A couple of types are available. One has parts—a flange and bar—while the other has the flange and bar in one integral unit. The latter is better. (See Figure 20–9.)

ACCESSORY QUALITY

Just as with other products for the bathroom, accessories come in varying degrees of quality. If you are buying metal accessories, solid brass construction is good, but for the long run—the money-saving run—chromed-plated brass will last the longest.

Carefully examine the finish of anything you're going to buy. It should be smooth and hard with a deep luster and free of obvious imperfections. If the finish is polished rather than pure brass, the accessory should have a clear protective coating to prevent tarnishing.

The best money-saving idea for accessories is to maintain them, but use nonabrasive cleaners. This will increase their life significantly.

Figure 20–8. The best kind of grab bar is one piece. Grab bars should be mounted on studs.

Figure 20–9. This type of accessory can be dangerous. It is an open invitation to grab when rising from the tub, or if you slip it might cause injury. Such accessories should be recessed in the wall.

Saving Money

Bath accessories are outrageously overpriced. It is suggested that you ask for a 25% discount when buying them, particularly if you're also buying a fixture or two.

Also, know what you're buying. There's no formula for doing this, but if you look at a lot of accessories after awhile the quality will shine through.

WALL, CEILING, AND FLOORING MATERIALS

Wall, ceiling, and flooring materials are often thought of as cosmetic aspects of a bathroom job—but they also must stand up to wear and be easy to care for. The chapters in this section will help you choose materials that are both attractive and durable.

21

Ceramic Tile

Ceramic tile is the most popular material for bathroom floors. According to NKBA surveys, tile is used as bathroom flooring 56.5 percent of the time; vinyl sheet flooring is used 42.5 percent of the time. For walls, however, other materials predominate: tile is used only 8 percent of the time as the main material. In any case, anyone remodeling or building a new bathroom should know about ceramic tile.

Ceramic tile is made of hardened clay. Depending on how it is made and finished, it is suitable for either walls or floors. There are so many different types, in fact, that it is easy to get confused when you go shopping. Our advice is to simply ask to see tiles suitable for a bathroom wall or floor, depending on what you need. What you are likely to be shown is detailed below.

WALL TILE

For walls, tile comes with a glaze coating that protects it against moisture. The porcelain or clay itself is hard but porous. The glaze may be gloss or matte (flat).

Wall tile is available in two basic sizes: $4^{1}/_{4} \times 4^{1}/_{4}$-in. squares or 6×6-in. squares. (See Figures 21–1 and 21–2.)

Most of the tiles that cover walls are called field tiles; these are the whole, or partially cut, tiles that abut walls, floors, or ceilings. There are also inside and outside corners, baseboard, and other trim pieces needed for the average job (Figure 21–3).

The availability of trim pieces dictates that it is wise to stay with American-made tile such as American Olean (the biggest), Dal,

and Wenzel. Decorative (and expensive) tile is imported from Italy and other countries, but you may not be able to get the trim pieces for it. Without the trim, the job really can't be done properly. American manufacturers make all the trim you need. Check before you buy.

Grout

Wall tile is installed directly on Sheetrock, Wonderboard, or Durock using adhesive. Pieces can be cut with a special cutter (Figure 21–4).

Once all the tiles—field and trim—are in place, a material called grout is swabbed onto the wall to fill the joints between tiles (Figure 21–5). Then the excess is swabbed off and the joints are smoothed.

Grout comes in many different colors and with or without additives to retard mildew. Mildew-resistant additives are a very good idea.

Take care in matching the colors of grout and tile. Some people like stark contrast, and that's the way it turns out: the grout dominates the job and gives it an almost stark look. It is safer to stick with a grout that is the same color as the tile: if you are applying almond tile, use almond grout or a complementary color, such as yellow or brown.

Some manufacturers make wall tiles in 12×12-in. sheets simulating standard $4^{1}/_{4}$-in. tiles with grout lines already in place (Figure 21–6). These tiles look good and are easier and cheaper to install than individual tiles.

Many people feel that a matte finish hides water spots better than a gloss finish does.

Figure 21–1. Design needn't be run-of-the-mill. Here 4¹/₄ × 4¹/₄-in. tiles have stripes made of contrasting color. (American Olean)

Figure 21–2. Here, ceramic tile is used artfully on wall and as a border for tub.

Maintenance

Both matte and gloss finishes are easy to clean, though some bathroom professionals prefer the gloss finish.

Money-saving tip: Using American-made 4¼ × 4¼-in. or 6 × 6-in. tiles will save you money, simply because they are standard.

FLOOR TILE

Floor tile differs from wall tile mainly in that it is designed to stand up to foot traffic; it wears well.

Floor tile has either a so-called crystalline finish, which is slightly rippled so that it provides a fair amount of friction underfoot, or a clear finish.

To find out how good the tile is, ask what the ANSI (American National Standards Institute) rating is. The rating goes from 1 to 5; the higher the number, the better.

Floor tile is available in a variety of sizes: 4 × 4-in. squares, 6 × 6-in. squares, a 4-in. octagon with a "colored dot," and a 4-in. hexagon with a colored dot (Figures 21–7 and 21–8). The 4-in. octagons or hexagons are interspersed with 1-in.-square (or larger) tiles of a contrasting color (Figure 21–9).

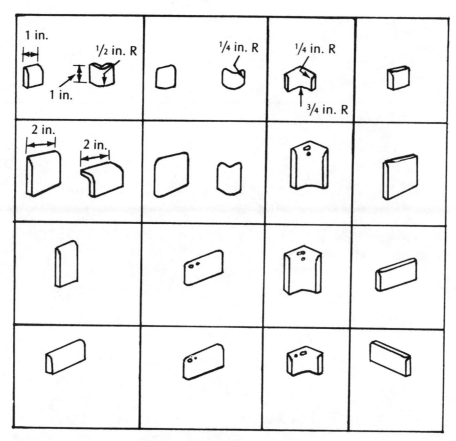

Figure 21–3. Trim pieces.

Figure 21–4. Wall tile (and floor tile) can be installed with cement or, as here—the much cheaper way—with adhesive. (Durock)

Figure 21–5. Here, grout color contrasts with tiles, but not so much that it dominates the view. (American Olean)

Figure 21-6. Different ceramic tile sizes can work well. Here, there are 4 x 4 tiles on the wall, 12" x 12" ones on the floor.

SHEETS

Ceramic tile also comes in sheets consisting of 1 x 1-in. or 2 x 2-in. squares fastened to a mesh backing. These tiles have an unglazed, flat finish that goes through the entire tile. You can also get 1-in. and 2-in. hexagons and other smaller sizes.

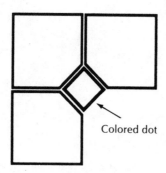

Colored dot

Figure 21-7. Colored or decorative dots improve the design greatly without extra cost or labor.

Tile sheets are most often used as flooring for a shower pan because they have no gloss and are less slippery than other types—and thus safer.

COLOR

Tile is sold according to color lots, and color lot A may be slightly different from lot B, even though the lots are nominally the same color. Some installers have gone halfway through a job only to discover that the tiles were from different lots—and so were slightly different colors. Make sure you have enough tile for the job from the same lot.

When you buy tile, it will come with a warranty. The warranty applies only if the tile is installed according to manufacturer's directions.

INSTALLATION

Floor tile can be installed either with a thick layer of cement (a "mud" job) or with adhesive or a thin layer of cement ("thin set"). If you have an old house with a very crooked or wavy floor, you may want a mud job because you can screed the cement level. This allows you to make a level base for the tile, a difficult thing to do if you use plywood and adhesive (thin set). Plywood should be used wherever the subflooring is flat so that the plywood can be laid flat.

SAVING MONEY

Installing floor tile the thin-set way can yield quite significant savings over doing a mud job. It can take a contractor half a day to put down the mud and level it. Figure on saving at least 25 percent.

A thin-set job on plywood underlayment can be quite secure. But do use a combination of subflooring and plywood that's at least 1 1/4 in. thick and glued and screwed together. As long as the subflooring can't move, the tile secured to it won't crack.

Figure 21–8.   Colored dots in action. They come in various sizes. (Eljer)

Figure 21–9.   Ceramic tile sheets come in a flat finish and are used on the floor. Glossy tiles are not used on floors because they'd be slippery when wet. (American Olean)

A way to get good design at low cost is to use one of the color dot tiles, either hexagon or octagon. This tile looks very good, yet you won't pay more for it than for standard tile. (Installation might seem labor intensive, but it is not.)

22

Paint and Wall Coverings

For bathroom walls and ceilings, two kinds of materials predominate: wall coverings and paint. Wall coverings are the most popular: according to the NKBA, wall coverings were used by 66 percent of their customers; more than 25 percent used paint, and the rest used ceramic tile and assorted other materials.

WALL COVERINGS

Once, when one spoke of wall coverings one meant plain paper, but today the term refers to a variety of materials including vinyl and coverings that simulate grasscloth and burlap. Only some of these coverings are suitable for the bathroom, however, because of the large amount of moisture generated there. (See Figure 22–1.) A wall covering that can't stand up to moisture well should not be installed in a bathroom. Indeed, even wall coverings that can stand up to moisture should not be installed unless the bathroom has a mechanical ventilating system. Moisture can attack and loosen wall-covering seams. (See Figure 22–2.)

For a bathroom that gets heavy use, only fabric-backed vinyl wall coverings should be installed. The walls should be primed (coated) with an oil-base primer before applying paste and covering. The oil-base primer prevents moisture from penetrating through the paste to the paper facing on the Sheetrock, which is usually the wall material.

If you are installing wall coverings in a bathroom that is used infrequently—where high moisture is not present—any wall coverings containing vinyl, or even plain paper, will work fine (Figure 22–3). Specialized coverings such as burlap and grasscloth are not suitable.

If any wall covering is being applied to bare Sheetrock, special preparation steps will also be needed.

Sizes

Wall coverings usually contain 36 sq ft of material per roll, but come in a variety of widths: 20½, 27, 36, and 54 in. wide; some foreign manufacturers measure paper in meters, and you get only 28 sq ft per roll. Wall coverings may be bought in one-, two-, or three-roll bolts.

Wall coverings come either prepasted or without paste. Prepasted paper is pulled through a water box to activate the paste. For unpasted paper, the paste must be applied to each of the strips. In many cases a professional paperhanger will forget that the paper is prepasted and will paste the strips anyway. Note that the proper kind of paste must be used depending on the covering being installed.

Saving Money

Papers can be more or less difficult to hang, depending on their design. The more difficult it is to hang the paper, the more the paperhanger will charge you. Since there are so many different patterns and colors available, you can save money by settling for something that is not difficult to hang but serves your aesthetic needs.

The "drop match" is the most difficult paper to hang, followed by the "straight across." Simplest is the "random match." (See Figure 22–4.)

Figure 22–1. For a heavily used bathroom where a great deal of moisture is generated, use only fabric-backed vinyl covering. Other coverings won't stand up to moisture. (Sanitas)

Figure 22–2.   How bold do you want to be? Wall coverings allow you to be as far out as you want to be. A variety of lovely border strips are also available. (Sunworthy Wallcoverings)

Figure 22–3. Many other types of wall covering—including plain wallpaper—may be used in a powder room or guest room where moisture isn't a factor. (Wood-Mode Cabinetry)

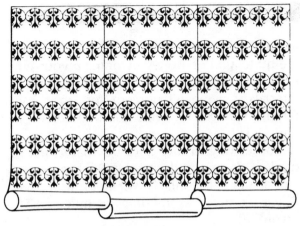

Straight-across match

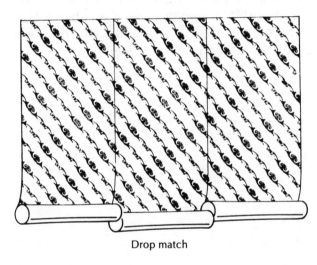

Drop match

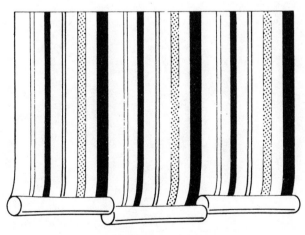

Random match

Figure 22-4. Wall coverings have degrees of difficulty in hanging. Drop match is hardest, random match easiest. There is also more waste using drop match.

You can also save by specifying that narrow rolls of wall covering be used rather than 54-in.-wide ones, which are more difficult to hang.

Another money-saving trick is to ask for a discount when you buy the coverings. Most retailers will give a 10 percent discount, just for the asking—and a lot more (50 percent).

Shop for coverings with patterns that are out of vogue. The prices of such coverings are often slashed 50 percent and more. (But be sure you can buy enough for the job.)

The traditional way to save is to do it yourself. Hanging wall covering, while not as easy as painting, can be a do-it-yourself job for anyone willing to be careful and patient.

PAINTING

In most bathrooms the ceiling and window are painted; in many cases, the walls are, too.

The key to selecting a good paint, as with most elements of the bathroom, is to get a material that will stand up to moisture.

There are two general kinds of paint for the job: alkyd, which has taken the place of oil-based paint, and latex, which is water-soluble. Both paints come in three degrees of shine, or gloss: flat, semigloss, and high gloss.

For the bathroom, the best paint is high gloss, because it is smooth and easier to keep clean than the others. On the other hand, it has a wet look—a high shine that many people think is too extreme.

Semigloss paint has a soft sheen and yet is fairly easy to keep clean. Most people favor semigloss.

Flat paint has no appreciative sheen and is more difficult to keep clean because it does not have a dense, shiny surface. It could be used on a ceiling, but not on any areas where it is likely to get dirty.

It's best to ensure that you get a good quality paint for the job. For our money, that means Benjamin Moore's top-of-the-line paint: Moorglo. (They also have paints that are not as good as Moorglo.)

Color

Moore, as well as other companies, makes paint in stock as well as custom colors. In selecting colors, remember that you are not going to get the exact shade you want. Paint on a wall looks a lot different from paint on a manufacturer's color chip.

Colors, of course, must be carefully selected for the bathroom to ensure that they work with your design. You might do well to pay a bathroom designer $100 or so to come by and give you an idea of which colors will work in your bathroom. Also, there are many publications with color photos that can give you ideas. Chapter 4, on design, also contains some ideas.

For the bathroom, most people, according to NKBA surveys, favor white (52 percent), with almond second (14 percent) and pastels third (14 percent).

SAVING MONEY

Painting is a labor-intensive job, so you can save quite a bit of money by doing it yourself. Perhaps 15 percent of the cost of the job is for materials, leaving 85 percent for labor and markup. That can be a few hundred dollars in your pocket.

Another way to save is to buy paint that is on sale. "It's one product," says Bill Lambert, a paint dealer in Laconia, New Hampshire, "that is always on sale—sometimes as much as 50 percent off."

Once you've decided what color you want—perhaps by visiting a local store and picking up paint chips—you can save time and effort by shopping around by phone. Different stores, you'll find, will have the same paint for vastly different prices.

23

Flooring

There are only two materials that are highly recommended for the flooring of busy main bathrooms: ceramic tile, which was discussed in Chapter 21, and vinyl sheet flooring. These materials make up over 95 percent of the flooring used.

This chapter discusses vinyl sheet flooring, as well as a few other floorings that are useful in some situations.

RESILIENT FLOORING

Resilient flooring refers to flooring that "gives" as you step on it. The two basic types are vinyl tile, which comes in 12-in. squares, and vinyl sheet flooring, which comes in 6-ft-wide and 12-ft-wide rolls of any length. The best choice for the bathroom is sheet vinyl, mainly because it can be installed in one piece, so there are few seams for water to work into (Figure 23–1). It is also generally more durable than tiles.

Figure 23–1. Seamless inlaid vinyl flooring. (Wood-Mode Cabinetry)

Figure 23–2. Another style of vinyl sheet flooring, this one from Mannington, a leader in the industry.

Figure 23–3. Carpet has limited use in the bathroom. Some designers won't use it because it's susceptible to staining. (Wood-Mode Cabinetry)

Vinyl Sheet Flooring

There are two basic types of vinyl sheet flooring: inlaid and rotovinyl. Inlaid vinyl comes in a wide variety of patterns and colors. Because the pattern and color go all the way through the material, it stands up well to wear. It comes in a no-wax shiny finish. (See Figure 23–2.)

Rotovinyl is not nearly as good as inlaid because the pattern and color are only on the surface of the material—they don't go all the way through. The wear layer comes in various thicknesses—the thicker, the better—and sometimes the rotovinyl has a urethane coating and/or a cushion backing.

Inlaid vinyl is normally cut in one big piece to fit the entire bathroom and then is glued in place. Rotovinyl can be installed dry—no adhesive—or with adhesive applied to the edges only.

As with ceramic tile, the key to successful installation is a tight underlayment or subfloor. There should be at least 3/4 in. of wood under a vinyl sheet floor, and it should be smooth, free of bumps, and screwed in place; screws are much stronger than nails.

Vinyl Tile

Vinyl tile comes in various thicknesses—1/16, 3/32, and 1/8 in.—again, the thicker, the better. Thin material wears out very quickly, and even well-known manufacturers make poor quality material.

Tile may be either the self-stick type or "dryback." Dryback tile is set into adhesive that has been applied to the floor with a toothed trowel.

Tile is not recommended for heavy-use bathrooms, but it can serve perfectly well in a powder room or infrequently used guest bathroom. Keep it away from close contact with moisture.

Tile is generally cheaper than sheet flooring.

OTHER FLOORINGS

Other floorings that could be installed in an infrequently used guest bathroom or powder room are wood and carpet.

Wood must be finished with a polyurethane or other water-resistant clear coating to protect it against dirt and vapor.

There are various types of carpet, but for bathroom use, we recommend only polypropylene, referred to as indoor-outdoor carpet (Figure 23–3). It can stand up to water fairly well. Like all carpeting, however, it takes a long time to dry if it gets wet. We suggest that you install carpeting loosely, so that it can be removed for laundering.

Carpeting quality varies, so take care to compare what's out there. The carpet may look good but turn out to be terrible. Like faucets, the beauty may be only skin deep.

One test is to grip the carpet in both hands and turn it back—this is known in the trade as "grinning"—to see how thick the pile or nap is. The thicker, the better. Also, read the warranty carefully and note what it promises—and doesn't.

COSTS

Install 4 1/4 × 4 1/4-in. ceramic tile on walls using "mud," metal lathing, "scratch" (first) coat, and average amount of trim:	$16.50/sq ft
Install 4 1/4 × 4 1/4-in. tile as above on Wonderboard or Durock:	$6.09/sq ft
Install 4 1/4 × 4 1/4-in., 6 × 6-in., or 8 × 8-in. tile using thin-set method or mastic on moisture-resistant Sheetrock:	$10.50/sq ft
Install ceramic tile accessories—towel bar, toothbrush holder, paper holder, soap dish, and grab bar:	$55.50/set
Extend ceramic tile above existing tile wall	
Using mud:	$16.50/sq ft
Using mastic:	$15.75/sq ft
Install ceramic tile floor as above, using mud:	$16.50/sq ft
Same as above using thin-set method or mastic:	$10.50/sq ft
Install inlaid sheet flooring over smooth surface using adhesive	
Economy:	$2.52/sq ft
Medium:	$3.05/sq ft
Premium:	$3.80/sq ft

For a 3/4-in.-thick plywood base, add $1.59/sq ft.

Part 7

HIRING PROFESSIONALS

Finding a good contractor to do the job is a job in itself. It takes work, and homework, but the payoff is huge: a good job at a fair price—not one that will give you nightmares even while you're awake. The following chapters tell how to do it.

24

First Steps

To hire the best possible person to do your job, the first step is to educate yourself about it. The purpose of this education is to give you a good idea of what you want, so you can communicate it to the professional. You don't want to be sold something that is not what you want, is of poor quality, or is too good for your needs. Remember that products and materials differ greatly in quality, even among brand names.

EDUCATING YOURSELF

Where do you obtain the needed information? Wherever you can. For example, if you are thinking of installing wall covering, read over the section on it in this book, then visit a wall-covering store to see patterns and examine the kind of covering you're interested in. You want to know exactly what it is. (See Figure 24–1.)

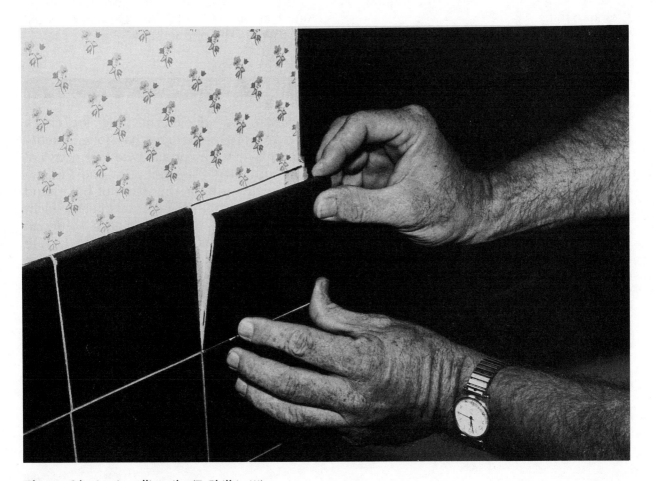

Figure 24–1. Installing tile. (T. Philbin III)

If you were having the entire bathroom done, your education would be broader. You might visit bathroom showrooms, go to ceramic tile outlets, view videos—do whatever you need to do until you get a very clear sense of exactly what you want.

NEED A PLAN?

In many cases—such as replacement of fixtures—you do not need a formal plan. You know exactly what you want, and no design help is required.

But in other cases—for example, if you are doing a remodeling job where fixture locations are being changed, or if a brand new bathroom is being installed—you need a plan of what is to be done, including specifications—a list of materials and products to be used. Then, when contractors bid on the job—and you should get bids—they all will be bidding on the same thing.

Where do you get such plans?

Architects

One source is an architect. While architects often work only on bigger jobs, they may well get involved in a small job, particularly in rough economic times. An architect will provide drawings from which the contractor can work: floor plans, elevations (front views), "sections" (side views), and plan details.

You should not just hire any architect. Try to find someone who is very familiar with bathroom design. You can contact the local chapter of the American Institute of Architects (see the Yellow Pages); they can provide you with a list of local people. You might also know a neighbor or friend who has had work done.

Generally, you can expect to pay $300 to $700 for a design from an architect.

One warning: many architects tend to overbuild—even though you tell them you're on a budget. Incredibly, only one in four projects designed by architects ever gets built.

Contractor/Designers

Another possibility is contractors who specialize in bathrooms. Some will prepare a plan; if you select them for the job, the cost of the plan will be forgiven or greatly reduced. If not, you'll pay full cost. (See Figures 24–2 through 24–5.)

You could also try a bathroom designer. We recommend that you get some names from the National Kitchen and Bath Association; they will have names of certified bathroom designers in your area. Some designers may not want to take your job because it's too small, but others will. A professionally designed plan—one a contractor can work from—costs from $300 to $500.

Some interior designers do bathrooms. Look for someone who belongs to the ASID—American Society of Interior Designers. You'll find them in the phone book.

CHECK JOBS OUT

Before hiring anyone for the design job, check out a few jobs the designer has done. The designer may have a certain style that does not fit in with what you want. Or—and this is a harsh reality—he or she may not be a good designer. The bathroom is an intense, high-design area that takes experience to design well. If a mistake is made it is made at the rate of well over $100 per square foot, the average cost for bathrooms.

Ideally, get someone with experience designing bathrooms. (Don't even consider plumbers!)

Once you have the plan in hand, you can go about the process of hiring the contractor who will do the work.

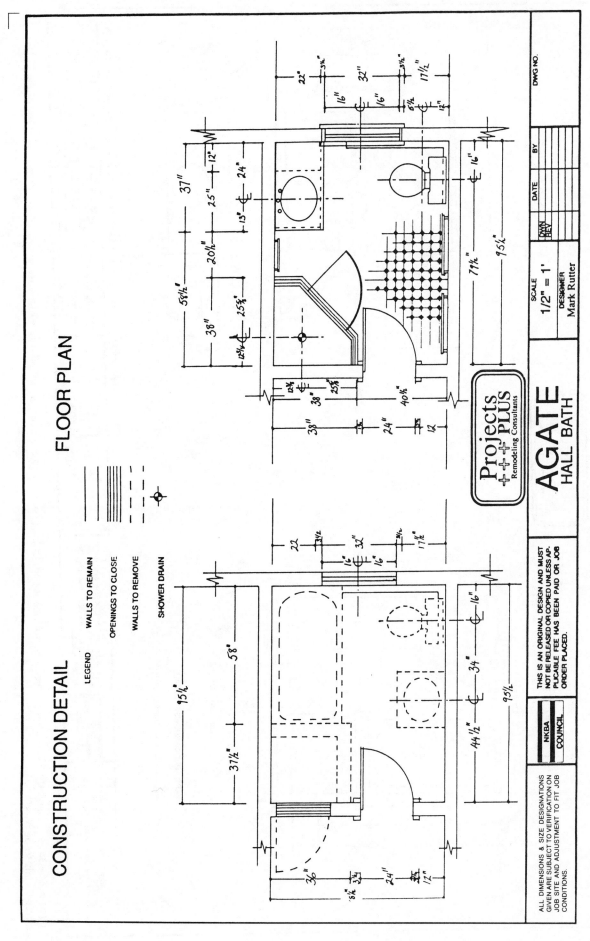

Figure 24–2. When you get a bath redone, floor plan is one type of plan you should see . . . .

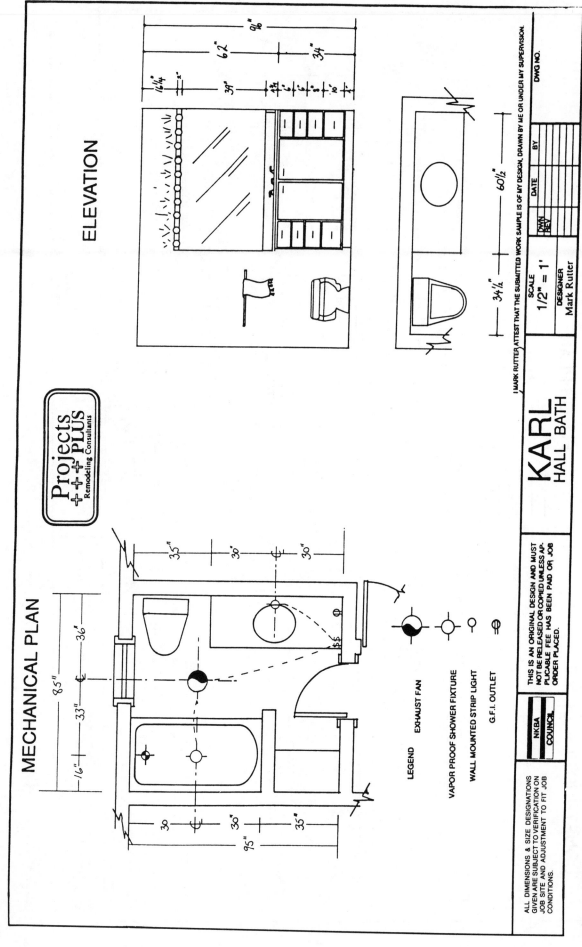

Figure 24–3. . . . and this is another. The contractor needs something specific to work from. Supplementing plans are detailed specifications of products and materials to be used.

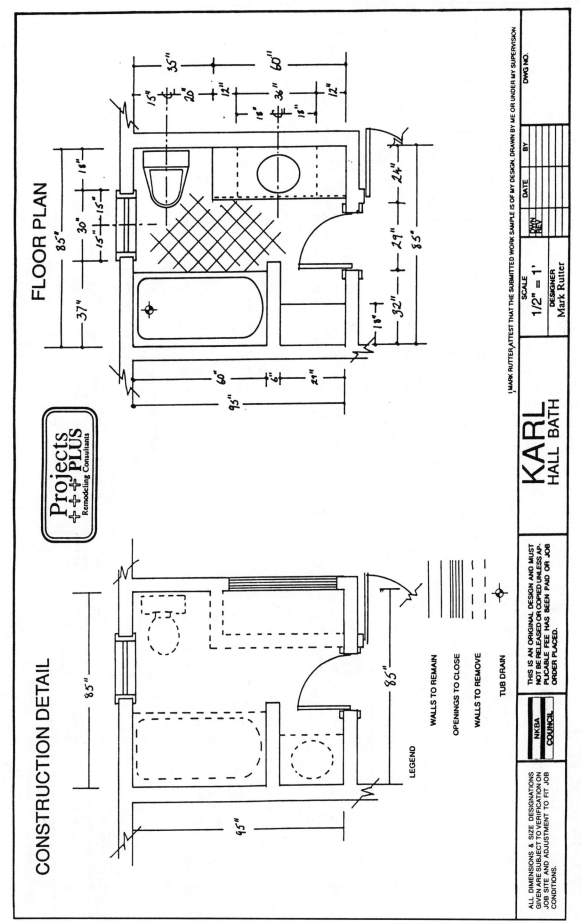

Figure 24–4. Floor plan of another job.

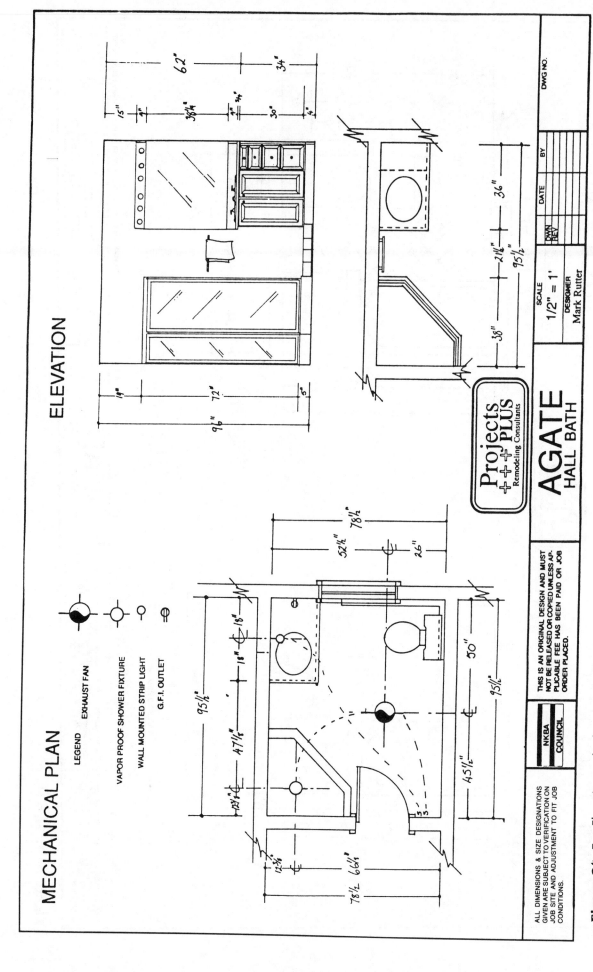

Figure 24–5. Elevation and other details of second job.

Checklist: Common Problems

To help you focus on what you need in the bathroom—assuming it's not painfully apparent—here is a checklist of common problems. Most have been discussed in this book, and you can refer to the text to get additional information.

Fixtures

- Is the tub big enough? It's amazing, but many tubs are not. A tub should be big enough to allow a single bather to stretch out and two bathers to be comfortable.
- Is the tub safe? Many aren't. They don't have nonslip bottoms or grab bars, or the faucets are difficult to reach.
- Is it easy to wash your face in the lavatory? Many lavatories don't allow this.
- Are faucets easy to operate? Some aren't.
- Is the toilet in a good location? One problem may be that the toilet does not have enough space around it. Fixtures were not designed to be jammed into small places.
- Are the fixtures the color you like? If not, they come in a rainbow of colors and many manufacturers make color-matched fixtures.
- Do the fixtures work well? Toilets should flush on one try, for example.
- Are fixtures easy to clean? Some are, some aren't.
- Do shower doors have tempered (safety) glass? Ask your local dealer. If it's regular glass the shower is a bomb waiting to go off.
- Do the faucets work well?
- Do you like the faucet style? If you don't, you're in luck. There are hundreds of different styles.
- Are fixtures and fittings worn?

Storage

- Are cabinets up-to-date or old-fashioned?
- Are cabinets in good condition? If not, they can be refinished or replaced.
- Is there enough space for grooming aids? In many bathrooms there simply isn't, and the grooming aids get lost in the medicine cabinet.
- Is there enough space around the lavatory? If space is cramped, an accommodation should be made for folks who are left-handed.
- Is there a handy storage area for shampoo, etc., in the tub/shower area? Most people balance shampoo and paraphernalia on the edge of the tub.
- Are there enough towel bars? Bathroom designers say that there should be 2 ft of towel space for each person who uses the bathroom.

Ventilation

- Is there a ventilating system in the bathroom? There should be. Not having one allows humid air to stand and can lead to all kinds of moisture-related problems, from drooping wall covering to peeling paint to rusting fixtures.
- Does the ventilating system leave the bathroom cold? Some exhaust fans change the air too quickly, leaving the occupants chilled.
- Is the exhaust fan too loud? Some are.

Lighting

- Does the light available serve all one's needs: reading, makeup, shaving? In some cases, people are getting by with one ceiling fixture and one medicine chest light, which they may be inadequate.
- Are outlets the GFCI type to guard against electrical shock?

Heating

- Is the bathroom chilly before or after bathing? There are heaters that can solve virtually any cold bathroom problem.

Design

- Does the room have a decorative theme?

Maintenance

- Are surfaces easy to keep clean?
- Are surfaces free of mildew and dryrot? If they're not, it usually means there's a ventilation problem.
- Do wall coverings or paint look worn and dingy?

Space and Traffic

- Can the bathroom handle family traffic? If people are waiting for long periods of time to get in it usually means a new bathroom is needed.
- Does the bathroom door interfere with any of the fixtures in the room?
- Are other rooms handy to the bathroom?
- Does the bathroom handle special needs, such as of older people or kids?

25

Finding Contractors

The best way to get a good contractor—and a fair price—for your job is to get several bids on it. This starts with a list of contractors. There are many ways to compile names for your list, and we will discuss a number of them in this chapter.

DESIRABLE SOURCES

The best sources for bathroom contractors are friends and neighbors. Why? Because they don't have a stake in your hiring the contractor.

Try calling people who have had bathroom work done—you want a contractor who specializes in bathrooms—and ask if they liked what was done and how the contractor performed. If the response is positive, put the contractor's name on your list.

Another source, though there is self-interest involved, is plumbing supply houses. Clerks will usually refer you to their best customers, and while this isn't an entirely objective referral—the suppliers want you to employ their customers so they will buy more supplies—the supplier doesn't want you coming back with blood in your eye or spreading the word about his terrible recommendation.

Other sources are kitchen/bathroom showroom people, real estate agents, banks (perhaps the one you borrow money from for the job), and the local Chamber of Commerce.

Local contractor associations can also provide names, but you should not take membership in an association as testimony that a contractor is good. Some are terrible. Associations are supposed to police their ranks but some don't, and even contractors who have

provoked hundreds of consumer complaints have been known to be allowed to stay in certain organizations.

Why? Because sometimes suppliers are on the committees that decide membership. How many suppliers are willing to alienate good customers, even though they may be dishonest or incompetent?

We don't mean to say that all associations are suspect, because that would be doing a disservice to the many good contractors in these organizations. But again, don't take membership as being equivalent to competence.

LESS DESIRABLE SOURCES

A less desirable source for contractor names is anyone who advertises. The logic is: If they're good, why aren't they in demand? Indeed, according to the Connecticut Department of Consumer Affairs: "Surveys in other states seem to indicate that homeowners who have hired contractors based on radio, TV or print ads . . . [or] the yellow pages . . . have more problems with their home improvements."

Here again, though, you won't necessarily get a bad contractor. Many good contractors, for example, advertise in January and February, when business is slow. Mark Rutter, one of the best contractors we have ever met—the consultant on this book—has been known to advertise in January and February.

Near the bottom in terms of desirability—they should be rejected outright—is anyone who comes to the door or solicits business on the phone. They have all kinds of slick pitches—including telling you they've done work "for your neighbor, Mr. So and So"—but they only know your neighbor from special phone books.

There is perhaps one other option that is the worst of all: hiring a friend or relative. The problem is not that friends or relatives aren't trustworthy, but that they may not be skilled enough to do the job. And if they get into trouble, what are you going to do? Fire them? It's a situation fraught with potential problems! For one thing, you can't proceed against a friend or relative without risking the ruin of your relationship. For another, you might have to hire a contractor to do the job right—and it will cost.

In a phrase, don't do it, as much as you may be tempted.

COMPILING AND WEEDING YOUR LIST

Most consumer agencies advise getting three bids, but we recommend that you get four or five. The list you start with should be even longer, because you'll be weeding out some contractors. A list of eight or ten contractors should be sufficient to begin the winnowing process.

To begin, check out the names at your local consumer affairs department and Better Business Bureau if your area has one (six states do not have BBBs in 1991). Consumer affairs departments and the BBB can't tell you if a contractor is competent, but they can tell you how many complaints they have received about the contractor and whether he or she is registered and/or licensed if the jurisdiction requires it.

Some good contractors will have complaints registered against them, but this doesn't necessarily mean that the contractor is bad. Some customers are simply "crazy," as one consumer affairs specialist said, and there are two sides to every story. Indeed, Bill Baessler, head of licensing at Suffolk County, Long Island, says that of each 100 complaints they get, 20 are valid, 20 are invalid, and the rest are "somewhere in the middle."

What you are looking for is not two or three complaints but a pattern. Incidentally, some consumer affairs departments and BBBs will not tell you the nature of the complaints unless you specifically ask. So ask.

Sometimes the BBB is impossible to reach by phone. Drop them a postcard to get action. Just be sure to give them full details on the company, address, and name.

LICENSED? VERY IMPORTANT

Many jurisdictions require that contractors be licensed or registered, and requirements for licensing may vary. Although in most jurisdictions licensing does not mean that a contractor is competent (California does require contractors to have four years' apprenticeship in a trade), a license does indicate some important factors (Figure 25–1).

First, it shows that the contractor at least complies with the law—he or she cares.

Second, it usually means that the contractor has insurance that will cover anyone injured on the job. (Incidentally, you can supplement your own homeowner's insurance with a million-dollar umbrella policy that won't cost much for the protection it brings; it provides for much more money in case of a suit than the standard protection available.)

Third, it may mean that the contractor is bonded (this varies from jurisdiction to jurisdiction). Bonding is a sort of job insurance. The contractor posts a bond, which may be forfeited if he or she does not finish the job.

Finally, when a contractor is licensed or registered, it gives the governmental authority involved enforcement power should the contractor not operate according to law. He or she can be threatened with loss of license, a fine, or even criminal action.

For all these reasons, it is important to determine that a contractor is licensed or registered. Licenses should be shown when the contractor comes to your home to begin work.

There is one other factor that can be absolutely critical. Quite a few jurisdictions have contractor refund programs. Under these programs, contractors contribute to a fund

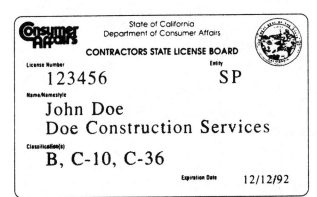

Figure 25-1.

administered by the consumer affairs department, the attorney general's office, or the local courts. These agencies will award refunds to consumers for jobs on which something goes wrong, for whatever reason. For example, the contractor may go bankrupt, run away, or refuse to pay for damage.

The crucial point is this: *These programs apply only to licensed or registered contractors.*

The sums awarded can be significant. In New York City you can get up to $20,000 per complaint; in Hawaii, $12,500; in Maryland, $10,000; in Virginia, $20,000; and in Suffolk County, Long Island, $5,000. In some cases you have to go through court and get a judgment, a process that is not difficult or expensive. In other jurisdictions, as mentioned above, consumer affairs departments or the attorney general's office administers the funds.

CALL CONTRACTORS

When you have pruned your list of contractors, call and invite each one to come in and look at the job. You needn't tell them that they're bidding competitively on a job—they will probably assume that.

Also, give them enough time. Call two or three months before you expect to see someone. Of course, they could come a lot sooner.

26

Getting Bids

You can get bids in a number of ways, but there is one way that we think is grounds for crossing a contractor off your list: he or she makes a bid by phone. If a contractor doesn't care enough about the job to look at it, how much can he or she care about doing it right?

TRYING TO LOOK GOOD

Any contractor who comes to your home has one overriding purpose: to get the job. In trying to do this he or she will, to varying degrees, try to look good.

Some companies do this with large books filled with color pictures of jobs they've done successfully. Their books will also contain letters testifying to the quality of their work.

If the company is big, it will point out its good service, its fiscal stability, and its large, efficient crews.

The small contractor, on the other hand, may tell you that he or she can charge a lower price because of lower overhead and because of not having to pay 9 or 10 percent to a salesperson. He or she may also emphasize the use of a permanent crew rather than a crew of subcontractors who possibly couldn't care less about the finished product because they have no stake in it being done successfully.

There is some truth in all these claims, and it is easy to get swayed or confused with people coming at you from all sides. Listen to what everyone says and consider it carefully. As time goes by you'll find yourself getting more conversant and more confident about which contractor you want to do the job.

FACTORS IN YOUR DECISION

There are a number of factors that will go into your decision. One consideration, of course, is price. Make sure that the bids you are getting are based on the same qualities of products and materials and the same work. This is why it's important for you to do your homework and decide exactly what you want before the contractor comes. Know the brands and models of fixtures, the kind of wall material, the specific ceramic tile, the lighting fixtures, and so forth. And have detailed plans to show. Then, when the contractors bid, they will be bidding on the same job.

Many contractors will not be used to bidding on jobs where the customer knows what he or she wants. Some may try to convince you that something else is better. If you've done your homework you'll know which option is better for you. If you change a product, material, or specification, you can lose control of the bidding process—you'll be taking bids on apples and oranges instead of on oranges and oranges. For example, if one contractor tells you that American Standard fixtures are better than Kohler, and you change the specs, what about the other contractors who made a bid based on Kohler fixtures?

Of course, a contractor may make a lot of sense and convince you that one product is indeed better than another. What do you do then? How do you find out if what he or she is saying is correct?

One good way is to check it out with other contractors, suppliers, or perhaps the person who designed the job. If the suggestion is valid, make the change. You can tell any contractors who have already bid about the change so it can be reflected in their bids. Then make it part of the job for anyone new coming in.

MIDDLE BID BEST?

You can expect to get a variety of bids, ranging from very low to very high. Indeed, thousands of dollars can separate bids on both remodeling jobs and brand new bathrooms.

Many people will automatically gravitate to the lowest bid. Classically, however, the lowest bid is the one to stay away from. A low bid may mean the contractor may have underbid. In essence, he doesn't know what he's doing. So once he gets into the job and realizes he's going to lose money, he may cut corners or leave the job just partly finished.

Each year, half of the home improvement contractors in the United States go under—a stunning 95 percent do so over five years—and the main reason is that they are poor businesspeople: *they don't charge enough money.* They charge just for materials and labor, forgetting overhead or what one architect calls "the wolves in the walls" (such as a gas pipe not figured on or a water or drain pipe or whatever). The contractor may also be desperate for the job.

A very high bid in relation to other bids may mean that the contractor is greedy—or that he doesn't know what he's doing, either.

Classically, the middle bids are the most realistic and therefore the best.

A good trick to keep things straight as you get bids is to use a form, as the one shown in the box, on which you can enter information about each of the contractors, comparing and contrasting what they have to offer.

Whenever you get a bid from any contractor it should be in writing. In many cases, contractors will have bid forms, but these are often not detailed enough (see Chapter 30).

OTHER SELECTION FACTORS

Unfortunately, picking a contractor does not lend itself to an airtight formula, so even a good price on a job is not reason enough to hire someone. Even if a contractor seems honest, competent, and reliable, he still may not be right for you because he has the personality of a wolverine and you're afraid to talk with him. Being scared of the contractor is a major deficit, because on almost any bathroom job something will go wrong or you'll see things you don't like. What happens if you can't talk with the contractor to make adjustments? You should feel comfortable talking to the contractor; if you don't, pass him by.

STARTING TO FOCUS

Once you focus on a particular contractor, ask him or her to furnish the names of *fifteen or twenty* recent customers as references. The contractor shouldn't object. Indeed, many can just print out names on a computer and hand them to you.

Also, get the address of the place where the contractor is currently working. Say that you'd like to see the work in person. Ask if he or she has workmen's compensation as well as liability insurance.

Once you have all these things in order, it's time to do the final checking.

Information-Gathering Form

It's a good idea to keep a written record of what each contractor who comes in to bid says to you. The information is easier to evaluate once it is down in writing, where direct comparisons can be made.

The form below can be adapted for your own job. This sample is for a bathroom job involving installation of new ceramic tile and replacement of fixtures.

If you have done your homework before the contractors arrive, you will be able to specify the materials and products you want and will be prepared to evaluate what the contractors say. The sample contract in the back of the book gives examples of the kind of information you will gather.

Date: _____

Contractor Name: _____

Contractor Address: _____

Years in business (over 5 years is good): _____

License and/or registration number: _____

Floor preparation: _____

_____

Brand, size, color, model number of floor tile: _____

_____

Method of installation: _____

_____

Preparation for fixtures (new underlayment, etc.): _____

_____

Brand, model, color of toilet: _____

_____

Brand, model, color of tub: _____

_____

Brand, model, finish of faucets: _____

_____

Brand, model of tub drain mechanism: _____

_____

Brand, model, color lavatory: _____

_____

Brand, model, finish of faucets: _____

_____

Wall preparation: _____

_____

Type of wall tile, size, color, model: _____

_____

Method of wall tile installation: _____

_____

Accessories (brands, models, quantities): _____

_____

Warranties (whose, and who services them): _____

_____

Length of contractor guarantee: _____

_____

Job start date: _____

Job finish date: _____

Total cost: _____

27

How to Check the Contractor

Begin by randomly selecting two or three names from the list the contractor has furnished and contacting them. In all your conversations with the contractor's references, try to keep the tone low-key, informal, and conversational, rather than inquisitorial. Say that you'd like to see the job the contractor did because you are thinking of hiring him or her. Most people are proud of their home improvements and will let you take a look.

At the site, ask about the contractor: Was he or she on time? Was the job started and finished as promised? Ask about whatever particularly concerns you.

Look at the job. Does it look like the kind of finished work you want?

Looking at one job should be enough, but you may want to check out one or two more. The more research you do, within reason, the better off you'll be.

JOB IN PROGRESS

It's also a good idea to visit a job in progress. You may not know much about construction (although if you've educated yourself about a job you may know more than you think), but you can at least observe whether a job is neat, clean, and looks like it's being done in a workmanlike manner.

One contractor consulted for this book suggests that you check the contractor's credit or have the lending institution where you're borrowing the money do it, if possible. Another way of doing this is to check out the contractor's supplier to find out if bills pare paid on time. Of course, a supplier may not want to give you this information, but some will. The way the supplier reacts may give you a clue as to what's going on.

If you find out that the contractor is having trouble paying the bills, you could get into a nasty situation if he or she quits your job after the supplies are on the site. Under the lien law (explained in detail in Chapter 30), you can be held liable for paying the supplier if the contractor hasn't—even though you have paid the contractor in full!

PLACE OF BUSINESS

One final check is to visit the contractor at his office, to make sure that this isn't the trunk of his car. You want to ensure that if you need to get in touch with him, you can—either by calling him or, if necessary, by visiting him.

The office may not be elaborate, but that's okay—it's the person that counts. If the office happens to be in the contractor's own house, it might not be a bad idea to notice how the house and grounds are kept.

Usually, it's better to get a local contractor—and one, experts say, who has been around for more than five years. Most bad contractors have trouble lasting five years.

If the contractor passes all these checks, chances are virtually 100 percent that you have a good person. But it still pays to write a contract that will protect you and give you peace of mind.

28

The Payment Schedule

Once you've found the contractor, you need a detailed, written contract that specifies a number of things. At the heart of the contract is the payment schedule. If you control that, you control the job; if you don't, you don't. It's that simple.

PAYMENT SCHEDULE

The biggest mistake you can make is to pay in advance. Many consumer affairs organizations routinely advise giving the contractor one-third of the total job cost up front (Maine says half), but this advice is fraught with peril. For one thing, you can give the contractor the money and he may never start the job. It happens all the time. Or the contractor may work a few days and then give up.

The way to avoid such problems, one might think, is to give the contractor a chunk of money up front, but only after the supplies have been delivered to the house. What could be safer?

THE LIEN LAW

In fact, this can be very dangerous. Most contractors operate on credit with suppliers. So the contractor can order the materials, which are delivered to your home, but then, for his own reasons—perhaps he's in trouble on another job—he can use the money you gave him for supplies to staunch a fiscal hemorrhage on that other job (or finance his divorce or bail his kid out or make the mortgage payment).

The danger is that under the lien law—and this law applies in all states—if the supplier is not paid by the contractor, the supplier can seek payment from you—even though *you* paid for the supplies in full! He can file a so-called mechanic's lien or construction lien against your house and property. Then he has a certain amount of time, usually 60 or 90 days, to "perfect" the lien—follow it through in court.

You may think you can win easily in court—the law seems insane. It seems insane and it is insane, but in many states *fighting won't do any good*: if the supplier proceeds correctly he will get his money—*from you.*

This law has wreaked havoc on people. Some people have had their homes foreclosed, and we know of at least one suicide.

The lien law is not totally bad in some states (such as New York), but it is always dangerous. As you get involved in the process of hiring a contractor, you should find out how it works in your particular state. (Some suppliers automatically file liens when they deliver the supplies.)

SUBCONTRACTORS CAN FILE LIENS, TOO

Just as suppliers are entitled to file liens against your property, so are subcontractors (or workers) employed by the contractor if they're not paid. Indeed, as a job is progressing, you should ask these workers if they are being paid. If they aren't, and then the contractor goes under without paying them, you may be liable.

As you can see, the lien law make it dangerous to give any money up front *directly* to the contractor. A large advance for supplies can be given, but only, it is suggested, under the following circumstances:

- The check is made out jointly to the supplier(s) and the contractor.
- The check is made out to the supplier.
- A bond is furnished by the contractor.
- A lien release is given to the homeowner by the *supplier*. (The lien rights of the supplier cannot be waived by the contractor.)

OTHER PAYMENTS

Payments for the rest of the job can be made in any way you and the contractor decide, except for one overriding stipulation: *Never let the contractor get ahead of you on the money.* If you do, you are vulnerable. If he has your money in his pocket, and problems develop on the job—or in his life—he may not come back some day. Yes, you can take him to court, and the district attorney will proceed against him—after handling the murders, rapes, robberies, and so forth that are part of his or her daily workload. If you have what will be the contractor's money, he will be back.

Many payments are usually better than chunks. If you are having a bathroom redone, you might make payments after the tearout, the rough plumbing, the electrical work, and so forth. Or in thirds or halves—after each stage of the work is *completed*.

HOLD BACK SOME MONEY

Some money should be held back for 30 days at the conclusion of a job to make sure that if problems develop within that time the contractor will be back to rectify them. Most consumer affairs agencies say that 10 percent of the total price is adequate, and that strikes us as about right if the job is substantial—say, $5,000 and up. But if the job is small—say, $500—then 10 percent is only $50. If a leak developed inside a wall, for instance, a contractor might not want to come back, knowing that if he does he will lose money. Holding a portion of the money is an incentive for the contractor to fix any problems.

A guarantee by the contractor—without monetary backup—is not enough. Money is the only thing that matters.

Before you give the money, by the way, the contractor should give you waivers of liens from himself, his workers, and his suppliers.

The final step before hiring the contractor is writing the contract, and we realize that all this might seem to be too much work. It isn't. It is a bit of work, but it beats losing hundreds or thousands of dollars.

29

The Contract

It is very important to have a detailed, written contract with whomever you hire to do the job. Aside from its merit as a written instrument to be used in case of problems—and the idea is to avoid these—a contract prevents misunderstanding. The agreement is down in black and white.

HIGHLY DETAILED

Any agreement you make should be highly detailed. Make no assumptions about any important item. The files of consumer protection agencies bulge with complaints from consumers, some of whom either did not have a written contract or had one that was not detailed enough. As an official of Connecticut's department of consumer affairs said: "Contracts are one of our biggest problems. The contract should contain not only what the contractor will do, but what he won't do."

Indeed, a contract is so important that many jurisdictions make it illegal not to have one, and the contract must include certain clauses. In 1991, for example, Connecticut is close to enacting a law that makes it mandatory to include start and finish dates on the job.

A contract consists of the central agreement plus all the other papers that bear on it: town permits to do the work, a notice of rescission, and much more, as explained later in this chapter. When in doubt, photocopy everything—and keep it readily available and together in a file.

WHOSE CONTRACT?

Most contractors—perhaps all—have their own contract forms, some of which may be

---

Who's Responsible?

Sometimes the person who designs a bathroom job makes a mistake but is not actually involved in the job anymore. He or she just made the incorrect plans! But the contractor, who has problems created by such plans, is involved.

The question is: Who's responsible?

Even though it was not his fault, the contractor should be. By accepting the plans, he assumed responsibility. Still, he may not see things this way, and it is a potential sticking point that could cause problems and should be discussed before the job starts.

Of course, if the designer is also the contractor, there's no dispute over responsibility.

---

bought at the local stationery store and then imprinted with the contractor's name. Others have their own contracts drawn up and printed. Many of these contracts are inadequate. Some do not cover points that should be covered and do not even have enough space to detail the job. Others favor the contractor.

Nothing done in the bathroom can be spelled out in a page or two. (Tip: You might want to use the contractor's contract as the basic document and then add typewritten pages to it.)

USE A LAWYER?

Most consumer protection departments usually say that using a lawyer *may* be a good idea. We think whether or not you need a lawyer depends on how extensive the job is.

If you are just having fixtures replaced, you needn't have a lawyer. But if the job involves gutting an existing bathroom or building a new one, there are enough diverse elements—from installing new fixtures to building walls—to make it advisable to have a lawyer look over the contract. This might cost you an hour or so of his or her time—$100 to $150—to make sure everything is included.

You can't get just *any* lawyer. It's best to get one who specializes in remodeling. Ask people you know who have hired lawyers to help them on jobs, or call the local bar association and ask them to furnish you with the names of three lawyers who specialize in home remodeling. Any lawyer you hire should have malpractice insurance, so that any mistakes he or she makes will be borne by the insurance company, not by you.

WHAT TO INCLUDE

You might want to check with your local or state consumer protection office to see if they have a model contract, but be aware that those we've seen do not include everything we think they should. Following is a list of clauses that belong in any contract.

1. *Name, address, phone number, and registration or license number if required.* You want full information so that you can reach the contractor if necessary. A post office box is not good enough, but if you did your homework in checking out the contractor, you should know exactly where the office is—and that it's accessible to you.
2. *A start and completion date for the job.* This is often a bone of contention. Even with good contractors you can sit around waiting for the job to start or for the contractor to come back to finish it. Make a definite date when the job will start and when it will end. Some people write a penalty clause into the contract, stipulating that the contractor must pay so much per day beyond the date he or she was supposed to complete the job.

3. *Detailed description of products and materials to be used.* This is where many contracts are very inadequate. They just don't have enough detail. It's not enough to specify "Kohler siphon jet toilet." You have to be very specific, including model number, color, and so forth—in essence, the specs must be detailed enough that anyone could go into a store, read them off to a store clerk, and get the correct product.
4. *Payment schedule.* You can pay in any way you and the contractor decide, but the essence should be that the contractor never gets ahead of you.
5. *Final payment.* It should be stated that final payment—of whatever amount—will be paid 30 days after completion of the job, but only if the contractor furnishes waivers or lien forms filled out by the supplier(s) and subcontractors stating that they have no lien claims against the homeowner. Again: Don't accept anything signed by the contractor waiving the rights of the supplier or subcontractors. Those rights cannot be waived legally by the contractor!
6. *Warranty statements.* Many products and materials have warranties, and different warranties provide different protections. The warranties should be attached to the contract and state who is responsible for servicing them. Incidentally, to be valid, the products must be installed the way the manufacturer stipulates in the warranty. If they are not, the warranty is void.
7. *Contractor's guarantee.* Contractors usually provide guarantees. This clause should state exactly what it covers and for what and for how long.
8. *Fees and permits.* Depending on the job, permits will be required from the local authority. This clause should say that all required permits have been obtained. The permits should be attached to the contract.
9. *Insurance.* The contractor should be able to prove that he or she has workmen's compensation, as well as

personal injury and property insurance; copies of the policies should be attached. You can also get an extra umbrella policy for a small amount that will provide you with millions of dollars of protection.

10. *Injury.* A statement should be made that the contractor is responsible if subcontractors, agents, or employees are injured.

11. *Changes in the contract.* As a job goes along, many people decide to change things—the color of the tile, the fixtures, the wall covering, or whatever. It should be stipulated that any changes—they're called "change orders"—will be written down clearly and made part of the contract. It's dangerous for the contractor to say something like: "It *should* only cost a few hundred dollars to do such and such." That few hundred has been known to become a few thousand—and without the specifics written down, you are in a dispute. Also, if you change something and eliminate something else from the contract, remember to *subtract* the cost of the eliminated items from the overall price. They are called "deducts." For example, if you change from one model Eljer toilet to another more expensive one, subtract the cost of the first toilet from the total cost. People have been known to lose a lot of money through not remembering to do this.

12. *Cleanup.* A statement should be made that the contractor will leave the affected parts of the house "broom clean." For a little extra money, you can contract to have the house left "maid clean."

13. *Unused Materials and Products.* Those in new condition can be returned to the store for credit; unused materials that can't be returned can be given to the contractor for a credit or disposed of at the homeowner's discretion.

14. *Notice of recission.* This is what is known as a "cooling-off period," and it is required under federal law. It says that at any time within three days from the signing of the contract you are entitled to cancel it. You can either mail the notice within that time or have it delivered to the contractor. To be valid, however, the contract must be signed at your home, not the contractor's office. Also, if you need emergency work, the notice of rescission can be waived.

15. *Arbitration.* If you have a problem with a contractor, you can take your dispute to the consumer affairs department, the state attorney general, or, if a small amount is involved, small claims court. In certain areas the BBB will also arbitrate disputes. But anything large, pursued through the courts, can get expensive. You can win the case but lose so much money and time on lawyers and aggravation that it's not really worth it. You've won—and lost. It is better to write in an arbitration clause stating that if you and the contractor have a dispute that can't be settled by other means, it will be settled by the American Arbitration Association. This group has offices all over the country, and settling disputes through them will be infinitely cheaper than going through the courts.

16. *Signed and dated by contractor and homeowner.* In addition to being signed and dated, there should not be any blank lines in a contract—draw a line through them. You don't want anything added later.

Once you have the contract in hand, you're ready to go. It will have been somewhat painful and annoying to do it all, but not nearly as painful and annoying as if you cast your fate to the wind—and fate comes up with a contractor who is a bad apple.

30

Where to Borrow the Money

Once you decide what you have to spend and more or less what you want, it's time to obtain the money for the job. There are quite a few ways to get the money, and it is worth shopping around if you have to—you can save hundreds, even thousands, of dollars. (Most people don't—experts say only one out of three does!)

Before shopping for a loan, however, consider using cash if you have it. This is ordinarily a very good way to go because you don't pay any interest or fees. Of course, you will lose any interest you would accrue from having the cash invested. Basically, you have to ask which arrangement will yield you the most money. For example, if you're getting 10 percent on your money in a money market account and can borrow from your employer at a lower interest rate, borrow from your employer.

UNSECURED VERSUS SECURED LOANS

Most people will have to borrow the money. There are many different ways to do this. Generally, loans can be divided into two types: secured and unsecured.

Secured means that the borrower has collateral, such as a house, to back up the loan. If he or she defaults, the property can be seized. Secured loans generally carry lower interest rates than unsecured loans, because there is collateral behind them. The bank is not taking a big risk in lending you the money.

Unsecured means that there is no collateral behind the loan. The lender bases the loan on the borrower's past credit history and the fact that he or she has the income to repay the loan.

In the rest of this chapter, we will consider the various kinds of loans offered and detail the advantages and disadvantages of each.

HOME EQUITY LOAN

This type of loan lets you borrow against the equity you have in your house. For example, let's say that you have a house valued at $200,000 and you have paid all but $40,000 of the mortgage. The equity—the part you own—is $160,000; this is the amount that you can theoretically borrow against.

In practice, no bank is going to let you borrow the full $160,000 because your payments—even on a thirty-year loan—would probably put an undue burden on you, based on income. Banks do not like to lend so much that the loan payment plus monthly debts exceed 37 percent. So, for example, if your monthly debts were 20 percent of your total income, you would be eligible at most banks for a loan that would add up to 17 percent more to your monthly debt.

Home equity loans are based on the "prime," also known as the prime rate, which is the rate at which banks lend money to their best customers. For example, if the prime rate were 9 percent, the bank might lend money to ordinary customers at 2 percent above that, but it could be 3 or 4 percent—(or "points"). Each percentage point, as you can see in the example given above, is significant. It depends on what rate the particular bank chooses to charge.

For some loans the interest rate is fixed, and for others it is adjustable (the rate can vary according to the prime rate). Getting a loan under an adjustable rate is about as sensible as shooting craps. You might benefit, but you can also take a beating. If you are considering an adjustable-rate loan, ask what the "cap" rate is (the rate above which the interest cannot go). Our advice is to avoid these adjustable-rate loans.

One big advantage of home equity loans is on taxes. As the law is written now, all interest charged is tax deductible for anyone as long as the total debt on one's home or homes does not exceed $1.1 million, hardly a problem for most people.

But there is a down side: the fees one pays for borrowing in addition to the points. Such fees can be as high as if you refinanced your mortgage and would include, for example, $300 for a title search, $50 for a credit check, plus points—each point being 1 percent of the face amount of the loans. For example, three points on a $10,000 loan would be $300.

Both interest rates and fees should be carefully compared when shopping for a loan. Banks usually charge either low fees and high interest or high fees and lower interest. For a short-term project, like most bathroom remodeling, the low fee with higher interest way is usually the way to go. But check carefully.

Home equity loans are often thought of as being designed for bigger loans, but there's no reason they can't be used for a bathroom job. Again, though, shop around for the best rate.

HOME EQUITY LINE

This is like a home equity loan in that you borrow on the equity you have in the house, but there are important differences. For one thing, you don't take all the money up front, as you would if you had a home equity loan. For example, say you were granted a loan of $20,000. Under the home equity loan you'd get it all up front. Under the home equity line, you'd get a line of credit up to $20,000 and then could borrow against that—$20,000 all at once, a few thousand a week, or whatever you choose—simply by writing checks.

One advantage of this type of loan is that you pay interest only on what you write the checks for, not on the balance available. This could be advantageous if you were making step payments to a contractor. For example, you might pay $9,000 over three weeks, but only $3,000 the first week, $3,000 the second, and $3,000 the third. You would be charged interest only on what you took, as you took it.

Home equity lines are the same as home equity loans in terms of interest, fees, and points—and tax deductibility. Again, check the cap rate on an adjustable-interest loan, and make sure you compare interest rates and fees.

Some banks offer so-called balloon payment arrangements. This allows you to pay only interest for a short period of time and then pay the principal—the balloon—all at once. This is dangerous. What if you can't get the loan because of tight money? Or what if you try to get an equity loan but the housing market has been so bad that the equity in your home has fallen? You could be looking at foreclosure.

Banks sometimes charge relatively small interest on the loan for a few months, then raise it. For example, you might have a 7 to 8 percent interest rate for three months, then it goes up to 16 percent for the duration of the loan. Avoid such "come on" deals.

Credit unions issue home equity loans, and their rates are usually better than banks'.

Home equity loans and lines usually have a minimum that must be borrowed. This is now $5,000, right in the ballpark for major bathroom remodeling.

Finally, check out home equity loans and lines at around tax time. Banks often lower rates at this time because borrowers find the tax writeoffs desirable.

MORTGAGE REFINANCE

You can borrow money to pay off the mortgage and then borrow up to 80 percent of your home equity. The same constraints based on debt and income apply as they do with home equity loans.

The rates on a refinanced mortgage are usually lower than home equity loans or lines, but fees are often so high that refinancing is not the most desirable way to get a loan.

Interest on refinance loans is 100 percent tax deductible as long as the existing loan was made after October 13, 1987.

HOME IMPROVEMENT LOAN

These loans carry a very high interest rate—15 to 18 percent—and a short payback period—five to seven years. You can borrow $1,000 to $20,000. Monthly payments, because of the short payback period, are high.

If the loan is secured by the house, the interest is 100 percent tax deductible, and loan fees are low—about all you pay for is a credit check.

UNSECURED PERSONAL LOAN

Because unsecured loans involve more risk for the lender, interest is higher—up to a whopping five points—than on a home improvement loan secured by a house. Also, there is no tax deductibility and the payback period is only three to five years.

HUD LOAN

These loans are offered by the Federal Housing Administration (FHA), and under the plan you can borrow up to $17,500. Interest rates are about the same as for secured home improvement loans, and fees are minimal (a credit check).

Various banks administer the loans for the FHA. The big advantage is the length of the loan—up to 15 years, double the maximum for a home improvement loan.

401(K) LOAN

Your employer may offer this type of loan. They let you borrow money at just a little above the prime rate and with no fees.

LIFE INSURANCE LOAN

You can borrow up to 100 percent of the cash value of the policy. Interest rates are low—around 8 percent—and the interest is tax deductible.

CONTRACTOR-ARRANGED LOAN

Contractors, bathroom designers, and others have contacts with banks and can arrange the loan for you, but this is ordinarily of no benefit to you because the contractor doesn't shop around as you would.

What Bathroom Jobs Cost Nationwide

The charts shown here indicate the vast differences in the cost of a bathroom job depending on where you live. The costs given are average and could vary up or down by 20 percent.

Also included are the percentages of your investment you can expect to recoup once the house, complete with the improvement, is sold. As you can see, adding a brand new bathroom is far wiser fiscally, at least in terms of payback, than is mere remodeling.

It is assumed that the master bathroom is 8 x 10 ft with ceramic tile and Sheetrock walls, tile floor, and new high-quality toilet, tub, and shower.

It is assumed that the full bathroom is 7 x 8 ft with vinyl flooring, combination fiberglass tub/shower, lavatory, and toilet.

Charts are courtesy of *Qualified Remodeler Magazine*.

Master Bathroom				Full Bathroom		
City	Cost to Construct	Value Added	Percent Recouped	City	Cost to Construct	Value Added	Percent Recouped
San Francisco (San Bruno)	11,010	10,000	91	San Francisco (San Bruno)	5,240	10,000	191
Los Angeles (Granada Hills)	10,285	4,000	39	Los Angeles (Granada Hills)	4,895	4,000	82
Los Angeles (Woodland Hills)	10,285	5,000	49	Los Angeles (Woodland Hills)	4,895	5,000	102
San Francisco (East Bay)	11,010	1,250	11	San Francisco (East Bay)	5,240	2,750	52
Boston	10,190	5,000	49	Boston	4,850	4,500	93
San Diego	10,285	1,500	15	San Diego	4,895	10,000	204
Chicago	9,375	4,000	43	Chicago	4,460	5,000	112
Baltimore	8,555	0	0	Baltimore	4,070	3,000	74
Minneapolis	9,375	2,000	21	Minneapolis	4,460	4,000	90
Las Vegas	9,740	1,000	10	Las Vegas	4,635	1,000	22
Kansas City	9,190	2,000	22	Kansas City	4,375	5,000	114
Miami	8,190	1,500	18	Miami	3,895	4,000	103
Milwaukee	8,920	7,000	78	Milwaukee	4,245	na	na
Dallas	8,190	1,500	18	Dallas	3,895	3,000	77
Houston	8,190	3,000	37	Houston	3,895	4,000	103
Detroit	9,830	3,000	31	Detroit	4,675	5,000	107
Denver	9,010	1,000	11	Denver	4,285	1,500	35
Atlanta	7,735	3,500	45	Atlanta	3,680	8,000	217
Charleston	7,370	1,500	20	Charleston	3,510	2,000	57
Phoenix	8,735	2,000	23	Phoenix	4,155	4,000	96
Pittsburgh	9,645	1,000	10	Pittsburgh	4,590	1,500	33
Tampa	8,100	5,000	62	Tampa	3,855	7,000	182
Mean	**8,869**	**2,893**	**33**	**Mean**	**4,220**	**4,155**	**98**
Median	**9,193**	**2,000**	**22**	**Median**	**4,373**	**4,000**	**91**

Form for Closing Costs

Just as it's a good idea to gather written information on bids for jobs, it's a good idea to gather fiscal information when you shop for money to be borrowed so that you can make direct comparisons. Following is a form you may want to use.

Closing Costs

Lender	Appraisal Application Fee	Points	Origination Fee
A	_____	_____	_____
B	_____	_____	_____
C	_____	_____	_____
D	_____	_____	_____

Lender	Introductory	Percent Over Prime	Lifetime Ceiling Cap
A	_____	_____	_____
B	_____	_____	_____
C	_____	_____	_____
D	_____	_____	_____

Lender	Annual Cap	Bank Attorney Fee	Years Line of Credit Available
A	_____	_____	_____
B	_____	_____	_____
C	_____	_____	_____
D	_____	_____	_____

Lender	Closing Costs on (figure)
A	_____
B	_____
C	_____
D	_____

With labor generally being two-thirds of the cost of a job, a lot can be saved by the do-it-yourselfer. (Stanley)

Appendix

Do It Yourself?

If you want to save money on bathroom remodeling, there is nothing like doing it yourself. On the average, the products and materials for a remodeling job constitute about one-third of the cost, and labor makes up two-thirds.

Before you begin, ask yourself which jobs you can do. This will depend, of course, on your skill with your hands and your experience. But it may also depend on local plumbing codes. As explained earlier, building codes are designed to ensure that people install things safely. Some codes will not allow certain jobs to be done by anyone but a licensed plumber. Other codes will allow you to do just about anything—plumbing or electrical work included—as long as you get the job officially inspected.

Incidentally, if you are planning to do work without a permit, and the job requires a dumpster of some sort, be aware that your neighbors may inform town officials that work is going on. It's best to follow the law.

Anything you do should be equal in quality to a professional job. If you can't do this, don't do the job. Some time in the future, should you want to sell the house, a poor job can reduce what you'll get for the house. For example, a potential buyer may love the house but be turned off by the bathroom, which features a ceramic tile job with uneven grout lines and sloppily cut tiles.

The rest of this section discusses specific jobs, with commentary on their difficulty and a tip or two for making them easier. You can also buy videos from Hometime. Many libraries carry a variety of free how-to videos and, of course, there is endless how-to literature in the form of books and magazines at the library.

PAINTING

Any job that can be characterized as cosmetic rather than structural is certainly a candidate for doing yourself, and number one is painting.

Semigloss enamel is usually used in the bathroom because it's easier to keep clean.

You can use a mohair (short nap) roller to apply it but a brush does a smoother job, and the bathroom is normally so small that a roller is overkill. Use a 4-in. brush for walls and ceilings and a 2-in. brush for "cutting in" corners and narrow areas and windows.

Proper preparation (written on the can label) and using good paint are the keys to a good job. For our money, the best paints you can buy are Benjamin Moore's top-of-the-line grades, Moorgard and Moorglo. Latex is a lot easier to use than oil-base and gives just as good results.

Be particularly careful about preparing new Sheetrock for painting. Follow manufacturer's directions to the letter.

HANGING WALL COVERINGS

This is another job that is purely cosmetic, but it is more difficult than painting. Proper preparation of the walls is required, and the paper must be hung absolutely flat and with precise trim cuts.

Two secrets of a good wall-covering job are to use a good-quality razor knife and to change blades frequently. Or use a single-edge razor blade and change blades frequently.

If you are hanging paper over paper and the existing paper needs to be removed because it is in poor condition, you can often simply grab a corner of each strip and pull it off. This only works if the paper has cloth or plastic woven in.

In some cases wall covering will have to be removed by steam. This is a messy job but is not mechanically difficult. Just rent a steam machine and use it as instructed, and you can have the bathroom wallpaper stripped in no time.

Take care, though, to get all the paste off—use plenty of warm water and sponges. If you don't get it all off, what remains can interfere with proper paint adhesion, as well as with wall covering: the new adhesive may interact badly with the existing adhesive.

FLOORING

The two kinds of flooring commonly used in the bathroom are ceramic tile and vinyl sheet flooring. Vinyl sheet flooring is nowhere near as simple to install as vinyl tiles, but it has no seams and this makes it a much better choice.

Sheet flooring comes in 12-ft-wide rolls. To do the job in the average bathroom, you have to cut a single piece to fit perfectly over the whole floor, with cutouts to fit neatly around such things as toilet bowls and sink legs if it's going into an existing bathroom. As you can see, it's not a job for a beginner. If you're installing sheet flooring in a new bathroom, however, it's a lot easier because the flooring goes in before the fixtures.

Ceramic tile is installed with cement or adhesive. Adhesive is a lot easier. No beginner should attempt a "mud" job.

Ceramic wall tile can also be installed by the do-it-yourselfer, but it is more difficult to do than floors. Various moldings come into play, and a lot of cutting is required at inside and outside corners. It is the kind of job that you should not attempt unless you have a fair amount of experience working with tools and the patience to do the intricate cutting required.

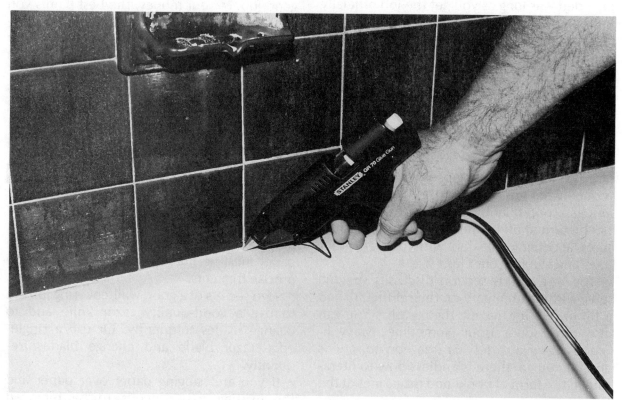

Figure A–1.   Simple repairs, such as caulking, can be done by homeowner. (T. Philbin III)

ELECTRICAL WORK

Electrical work that involves just replacing something—say, a standard outlet with a GFCI—is well within the province of the average do-it-yourselfer. Such devices come with instructions, and the job usually is just connecting wires of the same color to each other. An inexperienced person could also install a new light fixture in place of an old one.

Two cautions: You must make sure the power is turned off at the spot where you're working, and you should ask your local building authority—or your hardware or electrical supplies or hardware dealer—what work you are allowed to do.

PLUMBING

Unless you are an experienced do-it-yourselfer, don't try to replace faucets. While it is mechanically simple, problems can occur: if you don't get pipes connected exactly, you will get leaks.

Replacing a toilet is a simple job—just loosen the nuts, lift it off, and drop in the new one. But one caution: It must be put in carefully or there can be a gap where the horn or projection on the bowl meets the seal at the top of the waste pipe or closet bend, and this can result in leakage—a silent and invisible leak that will damage subflooring, underlayment, and who knows what else.

Replacing a tub is a job for a professional, as is running water and drain lines, unless you are very handy. If you make a mistake on pipes you can have a leak *inside* the walls, a very unhappy event.

Replacing a medicine cabinet is another job that the do-it-yourselfer can do, and installing shelves and various storage units is also relatively simple.

Repair First?

Many times bath items do not have to be replaced if the problem is just mechanical rather than aesthetic. There are all kinds of good products around that can make things that seem beyond repair eminently repairable, everything from caulking seams (Figure A–1) to renewing toilet tanks with a toilet tank repair kit (Figure A–2). Don't assume something can't be saved—assume it can.

WORK WITH CONTRACTORS?

If you are having a renovation done where you are tearing out an old bathroom, perhaps taking walls down, you may be able to work out something with the contractors: that is, you do the tearout (the dirty work), and they do the work where their technical expertise is needed. You can save substantial sums by doing this (10 percent or more, depending on the job), but you must take care to do the job exactly the way the contractor wants and to do whatever you contract for completely. If you contract to tear down walls and then leave nails in the studs, for example, you're not doing a complete job—expect the contractor to bill you for it.

Here are some jobs that even the relatively inexperienced person can do.

- Tear down walls. These are usually Sheetrock, and it won't take much to tear them down using a framing hammer. Have something handy for taking the material out of the house. Many remodelers use metal trash cans, filling them partway so they're not too heavy to lift easily.

Figure A–2. Some products, such as Fluidmaster toilet tank repair kit, can help you save having to replace a toilet.

- Remove fixtures. If you know how to turn off the valves, you can remove the fixtures. Just use pliers or wrenches as needed to disconnect water and drain lines, then plug them up with rags. Before taking a lavatory or tub out, though, make sure that the valves work. If they don't, water will spew all over the place when the fixture is removed. The best bet is to turn the valves off, then try the faucets to see if the water runs.

  The toilet and lavatory should be simple to haul away, but the tub is very heavy. A much better solution is to don goggles and use a sledgehammer to break up the tub and take it out in pieces. A fiberglass tub can be cut up with a reciprocating saw, but you must know where the supply pipes are first: it's easy to cut into these.

- Remove cabinets. They are usually secured to studs with a couple of screws.

Make sure that the contractor gives you an oath, in blood, (or a very tight contract) that he or she will arrive on a specific day to do the job. Some people have torn out the only working bathroom, and then the contractor did not show up for weeks. This is not an enviable situation.

One final tip: When doing any job yourself, be safety conscious, particularly with tearout work. It can be dangerous if you don't know what you're doing.

B

A Look at a Contract

This appendix contains a contract for a $10,000 plus, bathroom remodeling job. In this case, the anonymous contractor is very reliable and competent, but the homeowner still runs a risk signing it.

While the specifications for products and materials are good—because they are specific—the contract excludes such things as start and finish dates and who is responsible for possible injury. Most important, the contact contains a very dangerous payment schedule. The contractor gets the homeowner's money before arriving at the job—if he or she does arrive.

We suggest that you read Chapter 29 and then go over this contract. If should be enlightening.

Excluded here are permits and other papers that become part of the contract. The notice of recission is included. Plans are shown in Chapter 24.

Sample Contract

Connecticut Registration No.

Mr. and Mrs. Good Customer	555-2807	August 9, 1991
15 Windy Road		GOOD10
Thistown, CT 06903	Renovation of Hall Bath	
Ten Thousand Seven Hundred and Fifty Dollars		10,750.00

$2,000 is due upon signing of this agreement to hold time in schedule, $3,000 is due day work starts, $2,500 is due prior to sheetrocking and $2,500 is due prior to tile. The balance is due upon completion.

RENOVATION OF HALL BATH

ABC Company will only supply and deliver such equipment, material, and labor as described in these specifications.

Equipment, materials, and labor not included in these specifications can be supplied by ABC Company as extras at an additional cost for which authorization must be given in writing by the buyer.

All dimensions and cabinet designations drawn and specified are subject to adjustments dictated by job conditions.

When re-use of existing equipment is requested by the buyer, Projects Plus will accept no responsibility for appearance, function, service, or repair.

All surfaces of walls, ceiling, doors, windows, and woodwork except those of a factory made cabinet will be left unpainted or unfinished unless otherwise specified.

You, the buyer, may cancel this transaction without penalty within three business days from the date below. Please see attached notice of cancellation for further explanation of this right.

CARPENTRY LABOR

Removal of existing toilet, porcelain sink, tub tile, and wainscoting
Removal of all existing flooring and underlayment
Removal of all plaster behind wainscoting
Installation of approximately 20 square feet of CDX subflooring
Installation of PTS on floor over CDX subfloor in preparation for tile
Glueing and screwing PTS every 6 inches (every 3 inches at joints)
Installation of wonderboard to a height of 3' above tub on 3 tub walls
Taping wonderboard with fiberglass tape and mastic
Sheetrocking remaining walls where tile was removed
Taping all new sheetrock (3 coats)
Install Shower Rod, Towel Bar, Toilet Paper Holder, and Medicine Cabinet

CARPENTRY MATERIALS

1 roll plastic
5 lbs 12D common framing nails
2 4 × 8 sheets 5/8 inch underlayment PTS

 2 4 × 8 sheets of $\frac{1}{2}$ inch CDX plyscore
 3 tubes PL-400 Construction Adhesive
 2 tubes phenoseal
 2 Rolls R-11 insulation
 3 3 × 5 sheets $\frac{1}{2}$ inch wonderboard
10 4 × 8 sheets $\frac{1}{2}$ inch sheetrock
15 gal bucket taping compound
 1 roll perforated tape
.5 roll fiberglass mesh tape
16 lineal feet of $2\frac{1}{2}$" colonial casing

ELECTRICAL

Installation of 1 G.F.I. Receptacle
Installation of 1 Exhaust Fan
Installation of 1 Vanity Light

PLUMBING

Disconnect existing toilet, faucets, and lavatory
Rough plumbing for tub and tub and shower faucet in existing location
Install new tub
Installation of new shutoffs for sink and toilet
Trim new tub and shower valve
Installation of toilet, lavatory, and sink faucet
Includes labor, pipe, and fittings

ACCESSORIES

 1 Moen 3284 PC 1-H tub/shower valve, pressure balanced, volume control, push button diverter, HAF & tub filler
 1 Moen 4621 Chrome Chateau 1-M Metal waste, $1\frac{1}{2}$" conn., 4" centers
 1 Jado 862/008/000
 1 Broadway Shower Rod
 1 Baldwin 3013-260 Toilet Paper Holder
 1 Baldwin 3011-260 Towel Bar
 1 Wiltshire WB-3024-4 Silver Mirror

FIXTURES

 1 Kohler chrome tub waste and overflow
 1 Kohler K715 Villager Bath, enamel cast iron, with safe guard bottom, left outlet
 1 Kohler K-7160 Clear Flo $1\frac{1}{2}$" adjustable pop up drain

TILING

Tiling 3 tub walls
Tiling bathroom floor
Setting marble saddle in doorway
Install sanitary base tiles as transition from floor to wall
Grouting all new tile with white grout

TILE

  150 sq ft of American Olean 4 × 4 Polar White wall tile
   40 pcs of American Olean 2 × 6 Polar White trim tile
    2 pcs of American Olean 2 × 2 Polar White trim tile corners
   25 sq ft of American Olean 4 × 4 Chrystalline white floor tile
    1 Greek Thasos marble saddle 3.5″ × 30″ × ³/₄″
   25 cs American Olean 4¹/₄″ × 6″ Crystalline White (CR 365 white S-3419)

SETTING MATERIALS

  1 3.5 gallon bucket of A.A. quality wall and floor mastic
  1 25 lb bag of white A.A. quality plyset mortar mix
  2 10 lb bag of white A.A. quality wall grout
  1 sponge

CABINETRY

  1 24″ × 21 × 30 vanity white high pressure laminate European design interior to be low pressure laminate

COUNTERS

  1 24″ × 22″ × ³/₄ Corian top and lavatory in cameo white, drilled with a 4″ faucet spread

PAINTING

Painting walls above Wainscotting
Painting ceiling
Paint to be oil base enamel low luster

GARBAGE REMOVAL

All job related debris will be removed from job site

NOTICE OF CANCELLATION

Date of Transaction:

YOU MAY CANCEL THIS TRANSACTION WITHOUT ANY PENALTY OR OBLIGATION, WITHIN THREE BUSINESS DAYS FROM THE ABOVE DATE.

IF YOU CANCEL, ANY PROPERTY TRADED IN, ANY PAYMENTS MADE BY YOU UNDER THE CONTRACT OR SALE, AND ANY NEGOTIABLE INSTRUMENT EXECUTED BY YOU WILL BE RETURNED WITHIN TEN BUSINESS DAYS FOLLOWING RECEIPT BY THE SELLER OF YOUR CANCELLATION NOTICE, AND ANY SECURITY INTEREST ARISING OUT OF THE TRANSACTION WILL BE CANCELLED.

IF YOU CANCEL, YOU MUST MAKE AVAILABLE TO THE SELLER AT YOUR RESIDENCE, IN SUBSTANTIALLY AS GOOD CONDITION AS WHEN RECEIVED, ANY GOODS DELIVERED TO YOU UNDER THIS CONTRACT OR SALE; OR YOU MAY, IF YOU WISH, COMPLY WITH THE INSTRUCTIONS OF THE SELLER REGARDING THE RETURN SHIPMENT OF THE GOODS AT THE SELLER'S EXPENSE AND RISK.

IF YOU DO MAKE THE GOODS AVAILABLE TO THE SELLER AND THE SELLER DOES NOT PICK THEM UP WITHIN TWENTY DAYS OF DATE OF CANCELLATION, YOU MAY RETAIN OR DISPOSE OF THE GOODS WITHOUT ANY FURTHER OBLIGATION. IF YOU FAIL TO MAKE THE GOODS AVAILABLE TO THE SELLER, OR IF YOU AGREE TO RETURN THE GOODS TO THE SELLER AND FAIL TO DO SO, THEN YOU REMAIN LIABLE FOR PERFORMANCE OF ALL OBLIGATIONS UNDER THE CONTRACT.

TO CANCEL THIS TRANSACTION, MAIL OR DELIVER A SIGNED AND DATED COPY OF THIS CANCELLATION NOTICE OR ANY OTHER WRITTEN NOTICE OR SEND A TELEGRAM TO _____ AT _____ NOT LATER THAN MIDNIGHT OF _____.

I HEREBY CANCEL THIS TRANSACTION.

Signature: _____   Date: _____

Index

TOM PHILBIN'S

COSTWISE BATHROOM REMODELING

A GUIDE TO RENOVATING OR IMPROVING YOUR BATH

AMERICA'S TOP HOME IMPROVEMENT EXPERT TELLS YOU HOW TO:

- HIRE THE RIGHT PROFESSIONALS, OR
- DO IT YOURSELF
- SAVE MONEY AT EVERY STEP
- AVOID PITFALLS AND FRUSTRATIONS

$2.00 REBATE!

To receive your $2.00 Cash Rebate, complete this rebate certificate by hand-printing your name and complete address. Mail your rebate certificate together with an original receipt of purchase with book price circled to:

Tom Philbin's Costwise Bathroom Remodeling
Rebate Offer
P.O. Box 8124
Grand Rapids, MN   55745 - 8124

Print Name _____

Address _____

City _____ State _____ ZIP _____

Signature _____

This certificate must accompany your request. No duplicate accepted. Offer good in the United States and Canada. Offer limited one to a family, group, or organization. Void where prohibited, taxed or restricted. Allow 4-6 weeks for mailing of your rebate. **Offer expires April 1, 1993.**